Praise
What's Keeping Your Cu

MW00365184

"The toughest job in selling is not selling; it'
Cody and Harte's unique pain analogy no.
great reading."
  Al Reis
  Bestselling co-author of *The Fall of Advertising and the Rise of PR*

"The Dr.'s of pain have provided an antidote to most sales performance problems. This is a must read for junior sellers or those who have spent years in the trenches. Great selling is about understanding a client's needs, worries, problems, issues—and *What's Keeping Your Customers Up at Night?* hits at the heart of the key basic issues—and offers a how-to-do-it manual with many practical, real-life examples. The Dr.'s of pain have provided a prescription for those who are looking for a cure to their sales ills."
  Jerry Kaplan
  President, Magazine Group
  Meredith Corporation

"This book's message is not the traditional one. Cody and Harte don't exhort us predictably to get to the close or cut to the chase, but rather challenge us to build momentum and buyer conviction by, well, cutting to the cut. Their process identifies where the prospect is bleeding and then demonstrates that the solution to pain is the decision to purchase. We might call this 'customer-enabled' or 'customer-empowered selling' because, in a real sense, the salesman provides the customer with the obvious next step. . . the decision to be released from whatever it is that has been causing his or her pain. If you're a customer or prospective customer and have been up all night with a head full of woes, the salesperson who reads this book will know it. And believe him when he says relief is just a decision away. Your decision!"
  Bill Whelan
  Director of Training and Development
  Motorola Business and Government Solutions Sector

"A fresh and provocative look at selling."
  Ford Harding
  Author of *Cross-Selling Success*

"Customers buy things to solve problems, to reduce pain. The Cody/Harte book shows salespeople how to win by finding and fixing the customer's pain."
  Jeffrey Fox
  Founder of Fox & Co and bestselling author of *How to Become a Rainmaker*

"*What's Keeping Your Customers Up at Night?* will become the formula for all successful sales organizations, especially during difficult and challenging times. Steve and Dick have done a masterful job of combining proven successful public relations techniques with the concept of uncovering the customer's 'pain' to provide a unique selling strategy that works regardless of the product or service. The book is a must read for sales managers, trainers, and sales representatives who are serious about helping customers and prospects sleep better at night."
  Michael Colistra
  VP of Sales
  Thomas Regional Directory

What's Keeping Your Customers Up at Night?

CLOSE MORE DEALS BY SELLING TO YOUR CLIENT'S PAIN

STEVEN CODY

and

RICHARD HARTE, Ph.D.

McGraw-Hill

NEW YORK   CHICAGO   SAN FRANCISCO   LISBON
LONDON   MADRID   MEXICO CITY   MILAN   NEW DELHI
SAN JUAN   SEOUL   SINGAPORE   SYDNEY   TORONTO

The *McGraw-Hill* Companies

1 2 3 4 5 6 7 8 9 0 AGM/AGM 0 9 8 7 6 5 4 3

ISBN 0-07-141103-8

McGraw-Hill books are available at special quantity discounts to use as premiums and sales promotions, or for use in corporate training programs. For more information, please write to the Director of Special Sales, McGraw-Hill, Professional Publishing, Two Penn Plaza, New York, NY 10121-2298. Or contact your local bookstore.

 This book is printed on recycled, acid-free paper containing a minimum of 50% recycled, de-inked fiber.

Library of Congress Cataloging-in-Publication Data

Cody, Steven.
    What's keeping your customers up at night? : close more deals by selling to your client's pain / by Steven Cody and Richard Harte.
        p. cm.
    ISBN 0-07-141103-8 (alk. paper)
    1. Customer relations.   2. Public relations.   3. Selling.   I. Harte, Richard.   II. Title.
  HF5415.5 .C59   2003
  658.8'12'02373—dc21

                                                            2002154748

Steve: *To my mom, who always said I'd write a book.*

Dick: *To my three kids, Samantha, Steven, and Jessie, who gave me the experiences I needed to become a persuasive salesperson and father.*

Contents

Foreword

It's a strange time to be in sales. Because of the ups and downs of the economy, sales managers are sending mixed messages to the troops. On one hand, they espouse consultative selling, encouraging their reps to serve as educators to their clients, helping them to find solutions to their toughest business problems. On the other hand, they're encouraging salespeople to be more aggressive by setting unrealistic quotas or otherwise applying pressure that might spark them to revert to the arm-twisting tactics of the stereotypical used car salesman. We recently heard from one salesperson who left a flailing dotcom because he was told to embellish his product's capabilities in order to make a sale on the last day of a lackluster quarter. The salesperson did so, against his better judgment, and spent the next several months fielding angry calls from the dissatisfied client. He finally quit. "I felt like the guys in *Glengarry Glen Ross*," the salesman complained to one of our editors. "Because I was desperate to get the sale, I began to resort to pressure tactics. It felt sleazy, but I thought I might lose my job if I wasn't more aggressive."

Indeed, a 2002 survey of sales executives conducted by *Sales & Marketing Management* and Equation Research reports that 69 percent of sales managers have encouraged salespeople to employ more aggressive sales tactics since the economic downturn in early 2001, and 40 percent said they'd be more likely to fire a salesperson who didn't make quota. Yet many of the same respondents said that they valued salespeople with "product knowledge" by an almost two-to-one margin (66 percent) over those who were competitive (33 percent). Certainly, many managers are continuing to place value on a consultative sales approach as well.

Smart salespeople, of course, need both traits to thrive in this economy. They need to be highly aggressive—not by pushing products, but by pushing knowledge that will help their clients succeed. Unfortunately, although many pay lip service to the notion of consultative selling, few sales managers and salespeople actually have plans in place for implementing a consultative approach into their selling culture. Thankfully, Steven Cody and Dr. Richard Harte have dedicated this book to help sales organizations—and salespeople—do just that. Think of it as your own personal blueprint for becoming a true consultative seller. Becoming this type of salesperson, as you'll quickly learn, is much more than being able to ask your client a few questions, and provide a listening ear (which, unfortunately, is most salespeople's definition of "consultative selling"). As this book shows, you've first got to conduct a thorough assessment to see what's really keeping your customer awake at night. This can't be accomplished by simply asking customers to tell you what their biggest business problems are. Few prospects will open up and tell you their real worries when you've stepped into their offices on a cold call. The authors of this book have craftily combined the strategies of a sophisticated public relations audit with some good, old-fashioned sales techniques to help you uncover this vital information. More importantly, they tell you how to leverage this data smartly to gain a commitment to proceed from your customer. And they show you how to tout yourself as a consultative seller (again, using savvy public relations techniques) to those prospects whom you hope to convert into customers. You may be an expert in your industry, but how are you leveraging it? What are you doing to prove to prospective customers that you indeed are a valuable resource? There's much you can do to walk the walk, and you'll find many practical ideas inside. Becoming a true consultative seller is a daunting task. Fortunately, this book not only provides a game plan to getting you there, but it also helps keep you revved up as you make the transformation. (Let's face it. Even a highly motivated, hard-charging salesperson such as yourself needs a little extra jolt of inspiration now and then, especially in these uncertain times.) The last chapter, which shows you how to make dramatic changes in your life in just 30 days, offers goal-setting worksheets and tips on how to assess your progress along the way.

Put its strategies into practice, and you'll be a true consultant to your customers—which, despite all of the lip service paid to consultative techniques—is still a very rare breed.

Melinda Ligos
Editor-in-Chief
Sales & Marketing Management

Acknowledgments

We have a considerable number of people we'd like to thank, beginning with Denise Hamilton, Steve's trusty assistant, who dedicated enormous time and energy to typing and proofreading the book.

Thanks also to Deborah Brown, partner and senior director at Peppercom for her editing, support, and counsel on the book. Deb spent far too many weekends and nights keeping us on track and playing the role of "Joe Salesman," an anonymous, average sales guy who wouldn't know some of the strategies and techniques Dick and Steve took for granted.

A special tip of the hat to the various client sales forces with which we've worked over the past few years. They were uniformly open to sharing real-world examples of pain-based selling and extremely supportive of the book project (as we referred to it).

There were numerous others we need to pay homage to:

- Barry Neville, our editor at McGraw-Hill, who liked the initial concept, kept us on track, and pushed us as hard as we've ever pushed a client to ensure the book was as good as it could possibly be.

- Steve's partner, Ed Moed, who provided excellent feedback and never complained once about all the time Denise Hamilton was spending on the book.

- John Bellacosa, our crack 11th-hour illustrator, who brought life to our Silent Signals.

- Our wives and families. In particular, the lovely and talented Angie Cody, who made a couple of mean sandwiches for Dick and Steve as they labored through the 51st copy revision. And

Mary Harte, who persisted and supported Dr. Harte throughout the many changes in his career.

- Last, but not least, we want to thank Sam's Place, one of Manhattan's lesser-known eateries. It was there, over a bottle of Pinot Grigio, that we formulated the idea of marrying Steve's public relations techniques with Dick's sales strategies to create a new and different way to uncover and sell against a customer's pain. Sam: what's on the specials board tonight?

Introduction

While many salespeople have attended different types of sales training courses and read the best-selling books, few, if any, have discovered techniques to uncover the "pain" that is keeping their prospects or customers awake at night. Fewer still have understood how to leverage that "pain" as an asset in their selling. Virtually none have used their imaginations to sell. Nor have they mastered the concept of persistence. Furthermore, the subtle, yet sophisticated, techniques of successful public relations have *seldom, if ever before,* been used in a pure selling situation.

What's Keeping Your Customers Up at Night? is an exploration into how sales executives and salespeople can leverage proven public relations and imagination techniques to sell and persevere during good times or bad.

In *What's Keeping Your Customers Up at Night?* you see how this powerful, provocative, and proven blending of techniques opens doors and closes accounts that seemed beyond reach in the past. It will also provides the keys to deepening relationships and up-selling customers.

THE WORLD OF THE
TYPICAL SALESPERSON

There are many different types of salespeople. Two of the more prevalent kinds we come across are the following.

Grizzled Veterans
These old salts tend to be set in their ways, believe that most sales take place on the golf course, and are in greater denial than the *Fortune* 500

CEOs and CFOs who have been pleading ignorance in the face of gross financial misconduct. According to our qualitative research, some of the issues keeping them awake at night include: differentiating themselves, their companies, and their companies' resources; and remaining top of mind with the customers. Typically, old salts are very content with their roles within their organizations. They also tend to be quite content with their overall lots in life. They make nice salaries that support nice homes, luxury cars, country club memberships and all the other accoutrements. But in reality, they're probably only producing at 20 to 25 percent of their potential. When disaster strikes and a big account goes into review, the grizzled veterans become the proverbial deer caught in the headlights. They're scared, uncertain, and paralyzed. New approaches, while attractive in concept, seem as far away as the moon to these types of salespeople. If they do decide to go out into the field and forage for new accounts, they go about it in the same old way. Sadly, what worked 5, 10, or 20 years ago is no longer relevant in today's economy.

"Gen X" Types

These order-takers of the go-go dotcom days are typically lost at sea in today's uncertain economic times. They're ill-equipped to sell to a beleaguered customer with a decimated budget— a customer who's wearing multiple hats because she's handling the responsibilities of downsized peers and may be the next to go. These salespeople's pain points include time management and understanding how to build higher-level consultative relationships with customers.

Gen Xers have probably received some training, but after that, have been left alone to bring in accounts. As a result, they tend to suffer from separation anxiety. They're young and have no track records of experience to call upon. They're open to new ideas and approaches, but don't know how to tailor what they've just learned in a one-off sales training session. The classic example of Gen Xers at sea occurs in the life insurance field, where, after selling to every conceivable family member and friend, they come up empty in attempts to sell policies to the average Joe. This phenomenon typically occurs at the 18-month mark of a new salesperson's employment and is one of the major challenges facing senior sales management in the insurance sector.

Whether you fall into the grizzled veteran category, the Generation X rookie camp, or neither, our book will help. It improves communications between you and your customer, and takes you far beyond mere rapport building. You learn how to partner with your customers to find solutions to their most pressing issues. In the process, you master the customer communications process, which, when handled poorly, is the main reason why a sales process breaks down.

We walk you through a four-step consultative selling method that will open doors. We explain how you can use persistence and imagination to succeed. And we provide a 30-day road map to jump-start your specific situation.

So it doesn't matter if you think that the Back Street Boys are better than the Beatles or that Willie Mays was a far superior athlete to Barry Bonds. Whether you're a 30-year sales veteran or a green-as-grass rookie, you will benefit from *What's Keeping Your Customers Up at Night?*

UNCERTAINTY

Complicating the life of veteran and rookie alike is the speed and severity with which the recent economic volatility has impacted Corporate America. We're all dealing with three simultaneous villains:

- Greedy corporate chieftains who have mortally wounded such erstwhile stalwarts as Tyco, Global Crossing, Enron, and WorldCom
- Panicky individual and institutional investors who have pulled billions of dollars out of the market
- Global terrorism

Uncertainty has fueled record downsizings, which have in turn increased unemployment. The pressure to turn things around has never been greater. And guess where the pressure is greatest? On the sales force. Sadly, many sales forces have neither the skills nor the wherewithal to rise to the occasion.

But that's where this book will come in handy. *What's Keeping Your Customers Up at Night?* is based on the realities of selling in the new millennium. Plain and simple, it will provide you with the approaches and methodology needed to succeed in a *very* uncertain world. Literally every salesperson, regardless of the field in which he or she toils, will be able to benefit. Even you.

What's Keeping Your Customers Up at Night? is unique. It provides the best thinking from two experts in two different fields: public relations and sales training. Steve Cody is managing partner of Peppercom, a strategic communications firm with offices in New York, San Francisco, and London. Dick Harte is president of Harte Associates, a leading New York-based sales strategy and training company.

We'll give you a "sneak peak" behind the corporate veil to examine pain through the customer's eyes. In the process, we'll provide the savvy reader (that's you) with the keys to breaking the customers' codes by correctly assessing their pain and developing imaginative techniques with which to sell against it. We'll also present a five-act play called *The Pain Doctor* in which Johnny Salesman uncovers Suzie Customer's pain and then sells against it.

Fasten your seat belts. Place your seatbacks and tray tables in the fixed and upright position. We're about to take you on a bumpy, but exhilarating ride through the wonderful sales world in which you live.

What's Keeping Your Customers Up at Night?

CHAPTER 1

Uncovering the Pain

(Opening the Wound)

In the beginning, there was pain. Lots of pain.

Unhappily, pain has continued right up to the present day: There's a volatile global economy, terrorism, corporate scandals, and a lack of consumer confidence, to name just a few.

The watchword of the day is "uncertainty." And uncertainty exacerbates pain. In fact, the widely publicized stories we're reading and seeing about obesity are a direct example of uncertainty. People eat more when they feel like their lives are out of control because food provides comfort. The more they eat, however, the more out of control they get. It's a brutal scenario that can quickly spiral out of control.

Stress levels plummet when people address the sources of their uncertainty. There's even a name for this phenomenon. It's called the Zeigarnik Effect. Dr. Bliuma Zeigarnik's research proved that tensions build up whenever a task or goal is left unfinished.[1] The sooner we take strides towards achieving the goal, the sooner we feel better. It's true with weight loss, smoking, and yes, even sales.

Sales pain exists because salespeople aren't selling to their customers' pain. As a result, they aren't achieving their sales goals. And when they don't achieve their sales goals, guess what? Their stress levels go up. Figuring out how to achieve your specific goals will provide the key to personal and professional success.

"Sure, sure," you say, "but how?" By following our prescription. We're the pain doctors. We help you figure out how to set goals and achieve them. We teach you how to read a customer's thoughts, feelings, and actions, and use them to sell. Most importantly, you learn how to uncover your customer's pain, how to further open a wound, pour salt on it (yikes!), and then form a win-win partnership to ease the pain. Master pain, dear student, and you'll sell, sell, sell. And once you sell, the uncertainty and pain will go away. Life will be good again.

But enough pie-in-the-sky stuff. Let's delve deeper into pain. To master pain, one must first understand it. (Sounds a little mystical, doesn't it?)

Let's peruse a few recent examples of pain that we've come across in both the sales and public relations worlds. . .

No one understands my pain. Lots of salespeople come in and sell their products or services. Or they'll undercut their competitor to get my business. But, no one has ever asked what my problems and frustrations are.

The head of purchasing at a *Fortune* 500 retailer.

We've got a great company, but no one knows we exist. We put out press releases and some of them get published. But, it certainly doesn't make any difference for our salespeople who constantly complain that prospects don't know who we are.

The marketing manager of a top multinational publishing company.

My management is always asking me to come up with new ideas. They want new ways to bring customers into our stores. They want to outflank and outthink our competitors. While I see that as primarily my problem, I also see it as my vendors'. But, vendors come to me with products. They never come with out-of-the-box solutions.

The director of worldwide operations for a multinational private labeling and systems manufacturer.

I'm genuinely concerned that more and more corporations don't understand the value of public relations and think of public relations agencies as commodities. That type of mentality will end up with us competing with one another in auctions, with the low-cost provider being the only winner. You'd think we were selling paper clips or something.

The owner of a Midwest public relations firm.

While I'd love to be able to provide new ideas and new solutions to both customers and prospects, my company hasn't held a sales training session in more than a year. With the economy the way it is and my company slashing its budget, I can't see that changing in the short-run. What am I supposed to do?

A salesperson with a multinational media company.

Customers are angry and scared. They feel all alone with pressure from above and no solutions from the outside. Marketing managers are feeling heat from frustrated salespeople who want their prospects to know about their companies and their product offerings. On the flip side, salespeople aren't being trained to assess a customer's pain, and public relations owners aren't using their imaginations to think outside the box and develop new service offerings.

But the pain examples aren't just anecdotal. They're quantifiable as well. Peppercom recently partnered with a leading sales trade publication and the American Marketing Association to conduct two separate surveys. We wanted to know if salespeople knew what their customers' pain points were and if they had tailored solutions to sell against them. Guess what? They didn't, and they hadn't. According to a survey of 64 senior-level sales executives conducted by *SAM* (*Sales Advertising Marketing*) magazine and Peppercom, 81 percent stated that they have changed the way they sell because of the weak economy, but nearly half, 47 percent, still don't have a clue as to what's keeping their customers and prospects awake at night. Results indicated that while continued poor sales have led companies to step up efforts to satisfy the customer, there is still a large percentage of salespeople that isn't even trying to tap into their customers' pain. The most common strategies implemented by survey respondents to sustain and improve sales include spending more time on the phones (50 percent), increasing customer service (59 percent), and offering new services to customers (55 percent).

Further compounding the challenging selling environment is the disconnection that exists between the messages communicated by many companies' sales and marketing forces. In 47 percent of the companies polled by Peppercom and the AMA, the core sales and marketing messages are not the same. As a result, too many firms send conflicting statements to the marketplace.

So we have both quantitative and qualitative proof that there's a whole lot of pain and uncertainty out there. Pretty harsh, huh? Not to worry; our blended public relations and sales training techniques provide a solution.

PR TO THE RESCUE

Let's start with public relations. While we know that *you* have a total grasp of public relations and understand how it differs from advertising, direct mail, and all of those other elements of the marketing mix, let's quickly educate that palooka sitting across the aisle from you. You know, the one who got a little boorish after the flight attendant poured his first Dewars on the rocks?

While it is a multifaceted discipline, PR is primarily about generating editorial coverage. Studies have shown that readers, viewers, and listeners are much more receptive to editorial commentary than advertising, direct mail, or other marketing initiatives. Why? Because of the "c" word: credibility. When a reporter writes about a company, readers believe the words *much* more than the ones in an advertisement run by the same company. Editorial commentary is called "third-party endorsement," and it's powerful. It's not you talking about yourself. It's someone else talking about you.

Want to test this out? The next time you have an advertisement and article about your company, lay the two side by side in front of a customer or prospect and ask which one they believe more. Or look at it a different way. Suppose you've just met someone at an airport bar. The guy is middle-aged and about 30 pounds overweight. During the conversation, he tells you that he was the New York City high-hurdles champion while in high school. Believable? Maybe. But what if there was another guy sitting beside him who said that he went to high school with this big fellow, and yes indeed, the brute did hold some all-time records. It's more believable when someone else does your talking for you. And that's PR in a nutshell.

So public relations is the art of ensuring that a company's or person's image is presented favorably to the public. It's also the art of selling a company's benefits, via its products and services, to the media in order to secure a credible article in a newspaper or magazine. A variety of techniques, from developing key message points to controlling an interview, are used to obtain this goal.

Public relations strategies in tandem with our pain-based selling techniques can transform the most mediocre sales force into a world beater—one that is attuned to the customer and that can be managed for high performance. We call this blended offering the "thoughts, feelings, and actions," or TFA approach and, in this chapter, we explain exactly how you can use it to open new doors and form deeper customer relationships.

USING PR TO SELL

So, *why* is public relations so effective in a sales setting? It's so effective because you can use some of the same subtle sales techniques that PR pros use with the media to win over a prospect.

PR professionals sell stories to reporters. But to sell a story, one must be *really* good. Reporters are a cynical, jaded lot whose antennae are finely tuned. To interest a reporter, a PR pro must do thorough research. First off, he must know the reporter in question. He must read previous columns and totally familiarize himself with the topics that the reporter covers. There's no faster way to blow a story pitch than to call the wrong reporter and try to interest her in a company or subject that she doesn't cover in the first place. Assuming the PR pro does reach the right reporter and establishes his knowledge of the reporter's beat, he must still interest the reporter. How?

By differentiating the company, product, or service that he's pitching. How does he differentiate it? By quantifying the pain that's keeping his client's customer or prospect awake at night and positioning the company, product, or service as the ideal solution to easing that pain.

Here's a generic example from the world of public relations. We used to represent a dotcom that had contracts with many of the top retail Web sites in the country such as Nordstrom's, Neiman Marcus, and J.C. Penney. Their schtick was to provide a live customer service representative (CSR) to the online shopping sites of these retailers. Browsers could go to the department store Web site, and if they had questions, actually converse back and forth with this live CSR.

It was our job as the PR firm to deliver major publicity. We did it by first emphasizing the live customer service representative feature that the service provided. But to get major business media such as *The New York Times* hooked, we had to go a step further. We had to demonstrate a real problem-solution scenario. We had to demonstrate why a live person truly improved the customer shopping experience. Here's how we did it.

Everyone knows and loves Starbucks. In fact, one of their hallmarks is the in-store customer experience. But have you ever tried to deal with their Web site?

To demonstrate why retail Web sites, such as the one for Starbucks, need a live customer service representative, we brought a *Times* reporter to our local Starbucks. Naturally, the store personnel treated the journalist like a king. To set up our "compare and contrast" experiment between the in-store Starbucks shopping experience and the one on their Web site, we prompted the reporter to ask one of the sales clerks the difference between a café latte and a frapaccino. He received a polite, detailed response. Next, we asked him to log on to *www.starbucks.com* and e-mail those very same questions. Guess what? A week later, he still hadn't gotten a response. When he finally did, it was a one-sentence explanation. The bottom line is that the client received a major feature article in the *Times* touting the need for live online customer service representatives.

You can use some of our proven public relations techniques to become more successful in sales, and in your life in general, by learning how to do the following:

- Differentiate your firm.

- Differentiate yourself.

- Uncover the pain keeping your customer awake at night and leverage that pain to sell.

- Use the "problem-solution" approach in your selling style.

We teach you how to do each of those things in the next few chapters.

THE POLS DO IT

For years, smart politicians, global 1000 executives, and other thought leaders have leveraged public relations to understand their constituents' pain better, and to provide the strategic training and messaging needed to win audiences over to their sides.

The most successful politicians are those who understand the voters' pain. Remember Bill Clinton in 1992 with his message, "It's the economy, stupid.?" That campaign was all about grassroots polling. "Clintonites" uncovered voter unease, and then trained and messaged Bubba to assail consistently the Bush administration's economic record. By selling against the pain, Clinton overcame President Bush's post-Gulf War approval rating of 91 percent, and voters swept him into the Oval Office. (What he subsequently did in that office is best left for other authors to describe.)

Consider also the most successful business executives. The Jeff Bezos, Lou Gerstners, and Bill Gateses all demonstrated a profound understanding and anticipation of marketplace needs. Their companies provided product or service solutions tailored *exactly* to address those needs. (Whether antitrust laws may have been broken in some cases to dominate various markets successfully is best left for other authors to discuss.)

Selling to a customer is no different from selling a politician's platform to a voter constituency, or creating buzz around a new product or service offering.

The smart and successful salesperson (whether he knows it or not) uses public relations techniques to uncover a customer's pain, to differentiate his offerings, and to sell a tailored solution. He also uses PR techniques to convey confidence and reliability to a customer or prospect. And finally, he uses imagination skills to make his offerings so vivid and compelling that clients can actually *see* their problems being solved. (*Authors' note: Imagination techniques, which are discussed in more detail later in the book, are unique strategies and processes that allow you to envision your goal and understand how to overcome obstacles to attain that goal.*)

SHOW ME THE MONEY

All this hyperbole is nice, but you want to know (and we want to show you) how proven public relations techniques work in a real-world setting.

A global 1000 product manufacturer had successfully dominated its space for decades by selling low-end commodity items to the "who's who" of retail.

In recent years, however, the retail sector had changed dramatically. Many retailers were relocating their manufacturing facilities offshore. Others were consolidating their buying decisions. All were demanding creative ways in which to drive an increasingly finicky consumer into stores and outlets.

Our client saw a major storm brewing. Unless it could move rapidly up their customers' buying decision chains, its growth would flatten and profits would fall. Happily, the corporation had recently acquired a smaller competitor that dramatically expanded its range of services and products.

The challenge, then, was to reposition this company quickly and arm the sales force with what it needed to sell in a totally new and more sophisticated environment.

START WITH THE DIFFERENTIATORS

We began with a classic public relations technique called "positioning." *(Authors' note: We'll teach you how to apply this very same technique to differentiate you and your company from the competition.)*

Positioning starts with one-on-one interviews with company executives about strengths, vision, and areas of core competence. Next, we interviewed customers, prospects, former customers, industry analysts, and the media to determine the company's external perception. Finally, we took a look at competitors to see how they were positioning themselves; in other words, we found out what they were saying about themselves in the marketplace. When we were done, we'd created a brand new positioning for the firm that underscored its holistic, high-end consultative solution.

In effect, we transformed the corporate positioning of the company from its former product orientation to one representing a more global, consultative solutions provider. This positioning was distilled into one memorable sentence and rolled out to the entire organization, which in turn, communicated it clearly and consistently to all audiences.

THE MESSAGE IS THE MEDIUM

Once the positioning was completed, senior executives were media trained (another public relations technique) to communicate correctly and consistently the new positioning and key messages, and to learn how to control the interview.

Media training is a *very* cool thing. It mimics an actual CNN or MSNBC television interview and forces an executive to fine-tune messages to the point where, regardless of the question, she'll "bridge" or always go back to the desired positioning or messages. We PR types get to play the role of reporters. And typically, we ask tough questions designed to see how well an executive handles the pressure of an actual interview. You'd be shocked to know how many top managers can't describe their companies or explain what differentiates them. We've had clients shout, scream, and even cry during media training sessions. When they're done, though, the clients know that they're ready for anything a reporter may throw their way. (*Authors' note: Incidentally, we use this very same process to prepare client sales forces to assess and sell against a customer's pain.*)

With this particular client, we did the media training again and again until we were comfortable that the executive had the script down pat, was prepared for all possible questions, and was ready to "win" and control every interview opportunity. This is how you, as a salesperson, should feel about your sales calls. You absolutely must be bulletproof in preparing for every new sales meeting. How can you be bulletproof? You'll find out soon when you get to our meeting preparation checklist.

Finally, we sent our intrepid client executive out to meet the press and conduct interviews. His message: The retailing world had changed, and his company was uniquely qualified to provide high-level consultative solutions. In other words, instead of just selling widgets and features as in the past, the company recognized that it could provide broader solutions to a higher-level executive, and be viewed more as a partner than as a vendor. Articles in top trade magazines and business publications plus interviews on television programs began to create awareness.

In sales, *you* need to be ready for the first meeting. Make sure you've figured out how to position both your company (see our positioning questions that follow) and yourself (see Thoughts, Feelings, and Actions section later in this chapter).

HOW TO POSITION YOUR COMPANY

As we have mentioned, you need to position your company properly. Here are some questions to ask:

Internal Questions

(Ask these of your management team.)

1. How would you describe your company? (If you were at a cocktail party or in an elevator, and someone asked you to describe the company briefly, what would you say?)

2. Do you think this description will change in the next one-and-a-half to three years?

3. What are the greatest areas of opportunity for your company over the next one-and-a-half to three years?

4. What are your company's greatest challenges in the coming one-and-a-half to three years?

5. What are your company's greatest strengths?

6. What are its greatest weaknesses?

7. What do you believe sets your company apart from its competition? (*Authors' note: This is the most important question you can ask, since it uncovers points of differentiation.*)

8. How would customers, partners, or others describe your company; what is its reputation?

9. What would you like its reputation to be in three years?

10. What misconceptions exist about your company?

11. Discuss the three greatest customer benefits that your company provides (in order).

12. What is the company's management style? (How does the company conduct itself? What is its personality? Is it conservative? democratic? etc.)

13. Who are your primary target audiences? (Prioritize.)

14. Is there a company in your industry, or in any industry for that matter, that you particularly admire? Why?

15. If your company were to come to life as a person, would it be a man or woman, young or old, rich or poor? What kind of car would it drive, and what kind of music would it listen to? (This will help you determine the tone when you speak about your company. If it's a thoughtful, consensus-driven company, your tone might be soft and understated. If you work for the 800-pound gorilla of your space, you'll want to project a more forceful tone.)

External Questions

(Ask your customers, competitors, vendors, and others outside the company what *they* think.)

1. How would you describe my company? (If you were at a cocktail party or in an elevator, and you were asked to describe the company briefly, what would you say?)

2. Do you think this description will change in the next one-and-a-half to three years?

3. What are the greatest areas of opportunity for my company over the next one-and-a-half to three years?

4. What are my company's greatest challenges in the coming one-and-a-half to three years?

5 What are my company's greatest strengths?

6. In what areas might my company improve?

7. What do you believe sets my company apart from its competition? (Again, this is the key question.)

8. How would you describe my company's reputation?

9. What misconceptions do you think exist about my company?

10. Discuss the three greatest client benefits that my company provides (in order).

11. What is my company's management style? (How does the company conduct itself? What is its personality—conservative, democratic, etc.?)

12. If my company were to come to life as a person, would it be a man or woman, young or old, rich or poor? What kind of car would it drive, and what kind of music would it listen to?

Now compare and contrast internal and external responses. If they're in alignment, you should be able to formulate the core strengths and points of uniqueness into a coherent sentence or two that you can consistently communicate in sales calls and in your written materials. If the internal and external perceptions don't line up, go directly to your management to alert them. A more sophisticated branding and positioning project might be in order. (And we know just the firm they can call for help.)

Now, getting back to preparing for that first meeting with a new prospect, anticipate every conceivable question and have answers ready. Know how to "bridge" away from negative or irrelevant questions. For example, if someone asks about your company's recently deteriorated financial situation, it could easily turn into a negative conversation. Happily, you can bridge away from this conversation by stating, "Actually, what I'd like to talk to you about today is our new service offering. Your company is experiencing intense pain and we can provide you with the ideal solution." Be armed with the methods with which to uncover pain and to ease it with a tailored solution. (*Authors' note: See how to do it yourself later in this chapter.*)

So how can you differentiate yourself from your competition? Following is a checklist of what you should think about before you go on a sales call:

- *How can I differentiate my company from my competitors?*
  (If you've had the chance to conduct your own internal and

external positioning as we indicated, you'll know the answer to this question.)

- Is it larger?
- Newer?
- More established?
- Global?
- Swifter?

- *How can I differentiate my company's products and services?*
  - Are they cheaper?
  - Sturdier?
  - More flexible?

- *How can I differentiate myself from "average" salespeople?*
  - Do I know more about a prospect's industry and company-specific issues than other salespeople?
  - Do I know how to leverage resources such as the Internet, marketing collateral, and research reports?

- *Did I do enough research on my prospect?*
  - Have I read their annual report?
  - Do I know who the decision maker(s) is?

- *Can I present myself as a thought leader?*
  - Can I show the prospect a bylined article that I wrote?
  - Can I show the prospect that I was interviewed for a local newspaper? (*Authors' note: We show you how to become a thought leader in Chapter 5.*)

- *Is there someone I know in the company who can act as my "champion" and speak on my behalf? (Authors' note: We show you how to locate and nurture a champion in Chapter 4.)*

FILLING THE GAP

Having created the corporate positioning for the hypothetical company in the text, and having media trained the corporate executives and generated initial publicity, Peppercom then combined forces with Harte Associates to instill specific public relations techniques into a sales training format that would impact the entire sales process. Up until this point, the sales force had been perceived as order-takers. It was our objective to guide them towards a higher-level consultative selling approach.

We began with a version of our messaging process that we call "sales positioning." It begins with one-on-one interviews of sales executives and salespeople. In this instance, we asked many questions, the most important of which were: "What differentiates your company's offerings?" and "What do you think is keeping your customer or prospect awake at night?"

Simultaneously, we interviewed a host of customers and prospects. We delved into their vendor selection processes. We asked their opinions of retail vendors in general and our client in particular. Last, but not least, we asked what actually *was* keeping them awake at night.

Our findings uncovered a huge gap between what the client's sales force *thought* was keeping the customer awake at night, and what actually was. Client salespeople thought it was service, price, and delivery. While these factors were important, customers and prospects told us that they were crying out for senior-level decision makers—individuals who could provide counsel and make decisions on the spot—partners who could make the customers look good to their bosses. (*Authors' note: As noted earlier, we recently conducted a survey of 64 sales executives that revealed that nearly half did not know what was keeping their customer or prospect awake at night! Try selling a solution to someone when you don't even know what her pain points are.*)

Now knowing *exactly* what the customer pain points were and what the gaps were between our client's sales force and the customer, we went to work. First, we developed a preliminary script and message points that salespeople could follow that addressed the pain. Next, we arranged to piggyback on a previously scheduled global leadership meeting to arrange a day-long session with the senior sales executives. Our goal: Apply public relations and imagination techniques to help them break through and sell in a completely different way.

THE PAIN DOCTORS

Going into the training session, we knew we had an uphill battle: Most salespeople are a jaded lot. They've been through motivational training. They've been through Sales 101 workshops. They've basically had it up to here with "one-off" sessions that get them momentarily excited but no better armed to face the cold, cruel world.

Our client's sales team was no different. They'd been thrown into a new situation and were scared, frustrated, and generally angry at the world. They were expected to sell to a much more senior customer and to be successful right off the bat.

While *they* were concerned, *we* weren't. We knew that we had uncovered the customer's pain and could teach them exactly how to use our PR and imagination techniques to succeed.

We started by reviewing the internal and external findings of our sales positioning audit. We showed the salespeople what *they* thought their strengths and points of uniqueness were as well as what *they* thought was keeping the customer awake at night. Then we hit them with the customer, former customer, and prospect feedback. Talk about a wake-up call!

Many were surprised to see that customers were looking for *exactly* what the repositioned company would be selling. That was the good news. The bad news was the sales force had no clear idea of how to organize itself and begin selling the higher-end solution.

And that's exactly where we come in. We're the pain doctors.

We begin by assessing the pain. We do it from both the customer's and salesperson's perspective; this is crucial.

It starts with the big-picture problem: In this case, the customer perceived our client's salesperson as nothing more than an order-taker. To overcome that perception, we needed to apply some basic assessment and goal-setting tools. We started by identifying each side's thoughts, feelings, and actions.

What were the salespersons' thoughts? Well, they sure were working hard. They sure were being very sensitive to meeting the customer's most important issues: delivery and price. But their world was being turned upside down. They had to sell a much more diverse offering to a much more senior customer contact. And guess what. They hadn't received any training in over a year.

On the other side of the playing field stood the customer who thought that nobody was listening to her problems. Vendors weren't coming to her with new ideas. Her boss was breathing down her neck. Her job might be in jeopardy.

We next examined how each side was feeling. Guess what? The feelings were identical on both sides: frustration, concern, anger, and fear.

Finally, we identified likely actions that each side would take *if* the sales force didn't sell against the pain. Our noble sales guys would fall back into their old patterns and continue to sell against delivery and price. And what of our frustrated customer? She'll be out looking for a new vendor ASAP. In fact, the customer will probably cozy up to anyone who will listen to her and promise new, high-level solutions. See Table 1.1.

When we were done assessing the pain, the salespeople *could* see the big picture. They *could* understand the pain. They realized that they *could* use this pain as a selling tool.

With the assessment completed, we turned to the most important part of the day: Selling against the pain. This is where we leverage PR and imagination techniques to get the job done—to teach these salespeople how to sell against the pain. How'd we do it? Sorry, that's in the next couple of sections. Oh, you want to know now? Sorry. We're the pain doctors. Remember?

TABLE 1.1

ASSESSING THE PAIN

Situation/Problem to Be Assessed

Our qualitative research showed that the client's sales force was being perceived by the customer as little more than order-takers. Here's how we assessed the thoughts, feelings, and actions of salesperson and customer alike.

Salesperson's Thoughts	Customer's Thoughts
1. I'm doing my job.	1. The salesperson is not listening to me.
2. The company has not trained me to be a high-level consultant.	2. No new ideas are presented.
3. I'm too busy.	3. I'm looking bad to my boss.

Salesperson's Feelings	Customer's Feelings
Frustration	Frustration
Anger	Anger
Concern	Concern
Fear	Fear

Salesperson's Current Actions/Behavior	Customer's Current Actions/Behavior
Doing business as usual	Looking for a new vendor

HOW *YOU* CAN UNCOVER
A CUSTOMER'S PAIN

Sorry about making you wait, but we want you to learn our techniques in sequence. Before you can uncover a customer's pain, you need to assess yourself and find out what keeps *you* awake at night. If you're in pain and not sleeping well, you show up at work tired, disheveled, and grumpy. What kind of message do you think that sends to a customer or prospect? So that said, let's take a look at what *might* be causing you pain: Obviously, there's the mortgage, the kids' dentist bills, and that good-looking new neighbor who keeps eyeing your spouse. What else? What's causing you pain in your professional life?

Thoughts, feelings, and *actions* (or TFA) are the three fundamental psychological factors that impact any salesperson's behavior.[2] They're also fundamental to understanding your own pain.

How well you master these three areas will directly determine your success, or lack thereof, in the selling arena. In fact, thoughts, feelings, and actions are directly linked to your ego. If you don't believe that you'll succeed, you won't. Pure and simple. Everything in sales revolves around ego. Ego describes everything about *you* and how you feel about yourself. It also dictates your confidence and energy levels.

So let us ask you a question: How have you been feeling lately? Anxious? Depressed? Concerned? Indifferent? Each is a warning sign of some level of discomfort. Each is indicative of some kind of pain you're feeling. Remember when we asked you to create your company's positioning? Good. You'll also need to wrap your arms around what is keeping you awake at night. We do that because we want *you* to manage your own pain. The better you do at that, the better you'll do at managing your customers' pain.

Whatever your state of mind, you can improve it (and, correspondingly, improve your sales performance) by doing our little self-encouragement exercise. It's intended to help you override your built-in negative programming—that is, the way you've been looking at the world. We replace those bogus viewpoints with conscious positive ones that you direct. It's a practical guide to living your life and improving your sales performance by controlling your thoughts rather than reacting to the thoughts of others. It will help you focus. It will also help prioritize the truly important things in your life, and enable you to create vivid images of them in your mind. Those images, in turn, will help you achieve your goals.

Confused? Don't be. Give our self-encouragement plan a shot for 30 days and see if it doesn't help. (But be vigilant about it. Don't try the exercise once and give up. Do it every day for 30 days.) Read it. Memorize it. Say it to yourself at least three times every day. Day in. Day out. Use it in the shower. On the train. In the plane. See if your energy level and outlook on life don't improve dramatically. See if you don't become a better salesperson as a result.

Let's start by giving you a sample script to follow in your personal life, and two different ones that you can use in your business life. One revolves around your salary. The other concerns your customer relationships. Each will help you focus and succeed. *(Authors' note: A word of caution—do not practice these exercises in an automobile or while operating farm equipment. They're so relaxing that you might fall asleep.)*

Ready? Here goes. . .

MY DIET AND EXERCISE SCRIPT

(Authors' note: Repeat this script silently, or out loud, if you're comfortable with people staring at you.)

I feel calm. I feel relaxed. I feel in control. I am calm. I am relaxed. I am in control. I feel safe. I feel secure. I'm letting go. As I let go, all my muscle groups begin to relax. I feel calm. I feel relaxed. I feel in control.

As my muscle groups relax, all negative thoughts and negative feelings leave my body, leaving me with only positive thoughts and positive feelings.

My mind is now open to receive the helpful and beneficial suggestions I'm about to give myself.

I eat only those foods that enhance my health and energy level. I feel healthy and strong. I exercise daily for a minimum of 20 minutes and achieve my ideal weight easily and effortlessly. My eating habits improve daily. As they do, I experience the positive benefits in the way I look, feel, and act. Using self-encouragement daily allows me to persist until I succeed with everything I undertake.

Overeating and drinking is like putting poison in my body. I need my body to live.

I am in complete control of my eating habits.

I feel calm. I feel relaxed. I feel in control. I am calm. I am relaxed. I am in control.

MY "SHOW ME THE MONEY" SCRIPT

I feel calm. I feel relaxed. I feel in control. I am calm. I am relaxed. I am in control. I feel safe. I feel secure. I'm letting go. As I let go, all my muscle groups begin to relax. I feel calm. I feel relaxed. I feel in control.

As my muscle groups relax, all negative thoughts and negative feelings leave my body. Leaving me with only positive thoughts and positive feelings.

My mind is now open to receive the helpful and beneficial suggestions I'm about to give myself.

I easily reach my income goals by planning my weekly sales schedule in advance. I enjoy making money and increasing my financial assets each year. I constantly make progress and always know how I am doing. I update my financial goals quarterly and I am deserving of the financial success I achieve.

I am a responsible person and set aside a regular amount for investments and savings from each paycheck.

I feel calm. I feel relaxed. I feel in control. I am calm. I am relaxed. I am in control.

MY SALES SCRIPT

I feel calm. I feel relaxed. I feel in control. I am calm. I am relaxed. I am in control. I feel safe. I feel secure. I'm letting go. As I let go, all my muscle groups begin to relax. I feel calm. I feel relaxed. I feel in control.

As my muscle groups relax, all negative thoughts and negative feelings leave my body. Leaving me with only positive thoughts and positive feelings.

My mind is now open to receive the helpful and beneficial suggestions I'm about to give myself.

I feel good about myself as a professional salesperson. I am well prepared, relaxed, confident, and enthusiastic. My positive energy level is infectious, and my customers and prospects enjoy being with me. I am well organized and "plan my work and work my plan" daily.

I am especially skilled at using the telephone to get commitments. I am constantly researching bigger and better customers every day. I adapt my selling skills to each prospect, and I'm continuously asking tough questions to uncover my prospect's pain points. I am a good listener, and once I've analyzed my prospect's pain, I am willing to take the necessary risks to enhance the pain and provide creative solutions in order to get a commitment to move forward.

I continue to find better ways to sell my prospects and customers, and as a result, I am more successful than ever.

I feel calm. I feel relaxed. I feel in control. I am calm. I am relaxed. I am in control.

(Authors' note: Take these models and adapt them to meet your specific lifestyle and selling needs. Maybe you want to reinforce all the good things about a new relationship. Maybe you want to encourage yourself to learn a new language or to play bridge. Maybe you want to close a big, new account. Whatever it is, our self-encouragement script will work . . . if you use it and repeat it every day.)

WELCOME TO YOUR WORLD

All right. You should be feeling a little better now that you have your own self-encouragement script.

Now let's go even deeper. Let's focus on your sales world. We'll start by exploring your daily activities and how you manage yourself.

Answer these questions honestly:

1. **Thoughts:** Are you organized?

   - I believe that I follow a routine that doesn't vary much from day to day.

   - My life is chaos, so there is no way to prepare for each day. Flexibility is key.

2. **Feelings:** What are your feelings about your time management skills?

- I feel confident because I'm in control.

- I'm concerned because things are starting to get out of hand.

- I'm frustrated because I feel out of control.

3. **Actions**: What are you doing to correct your current time management challenges?

   - Very little. I try to prioritize, but I can't seem to stay ahead of the curve.

   - I create a "to do" list that is prioritized each morning.

   - I'm stuck in neutral.

   - I'm taking risks. I know I have to change things and have been trying something different each day.

If you're honest in your responses, you'll know whether time management is a personal strength or weakness. If it is a weakness, our book provides advice on how to make improvements.

Next, let's pretend that your company's sales are down and that support and training within your sales organization are somewhat spotty. (OK, fine. The sales organization is in chaos and you get zero support from headquarters. Is that more like it? Are you happy now?)

Let's get you to answer a few questions about your company. In doing so, we probe some additional thoughts, feelings, and actions:

1. **Thoughts**: Are you confident that you understand your company's messages, services, and points of differentiation?

   - Yes.

   - No.

   - Are you kidding?

Are you confident that you can differentiate your company from its competitors and yourself from the competitor's salesperson who calls on the very same prospects?

- Yes.
- No.
- Are you kidding?

Are you confident that you know what's keeping your customer awake at night?

- Yes.
- No.
- Are you kidding?

2. **Feelings**: What are your feelings about your company's sales situation?
   - Confident.
   - Concerned.
   - Scared.

What are your feelings about your job security?

- Confident.
- Concerned.
- Scared.

3. **Actions**: What are you doing to change the current situation?
   - I'm taking sales courses and reading books like this one to improve myself.
   - I'm wining and dining my customers. It's the tried-and-true method.
   - I'm making more sales calls. It's a numbers game.
   - I'm looking for a new career. Being a salesperson is a one-way ticket to Palookaville.
   - I'm doing absolutely nothing. Things have to get better.

All right. Now that we've made you feel even worse, let's help you figure out how to make your customer feel the same way (with the goal being to use that pain to sell). Besides, misery loves company, right?

Here's a typical situation our clients encounter: The customer's company has been in a downward spiral for the past 12 months. They've announced several rounds of layoffs, closed a bunch of plants, and taken all sorts of draconian measures to cut costs. The stock price has plummeted, and morale just plain stinks.

The customer contact is now wearing three hats: sales, marketing, and merchandising. She has agreed to meet with you for a half-hour to discuss your company's offerings.

Let's explore how you can use the TFA approach to uncover the customer's pain points and provide the information necessary to go beyond rapport building to actually sell against her pain.

TFA questions will differentiate you from the average salesperson. While they're intended to probe a customer's pain points, it's important to keep them nonjudgmental. For example, when probing a customer's thoughts about her company's poor performance, don't editorialize by saying, "I know your company is really struggling right now, and that has to be frustrating for you." (This is a typical ploy many sales experts suggest you use to build rapport.) Instead, frame the question in a nonjudgmental way, such as, "What are your thoughts about the company's performance to date?" See the difference? Can you see how the last question might elicit a more meaningful response?

Here's some specific advice that you can follow to uncover your customer's thoughts, feelings, and actions:

Thoughts. Your customer's world is constantly changing. To stay current and top of mind with your customer, you can use the TFA approach. (*Authors' note: You may recall that "remaining top of mind with the customer" was a key pain point identified by the "old salt" veteran salespeople we interviewed.*) For example, if your customer's main concern (pain point) is making sure she looks good in front of her boss, then probing for other thoughts would be useless. Your attention should stay focused on this particular issue, and specifically, how you can help her.

So, when she brings up the importance of looking good in front of the boss, be prepared to ask, "Could you share your thoughts with me?" That one question can provide a wealth of additional detail that you could use to make her look good (and develop a deeper relationship in the process).

Feelings. The ability to make an emotional connection in a sales setting is not unlike falling in love in your personal life. Connections in business, and in life, occur when you convince someone that you share the same exact feeling.

To illustrate what we mean, let's say your customer is frustrated with a vendor's chronic unreliability. You can align your feelings with hers by sharing a similar story from your life that's caused you the same degree of angst. In so doing, you've demonstrated you understand her feelings and would like to partner with her to solve the problem. While creating empathy is great, it usually isn't enough. We'll show you how to go beyond empathy to create pain and build a connection.

Actions. Believe it or not, a customer's actions can often be in direct conflict with her thoughts and feelings. We've often encountered a variation on the following theme: A customer will have used the same vendor for many years. But over time, service and quality have slipped. Although she thinks it's time for a change and is frustrated by the vendor's poor quality, the customer may be afraid to take action for a variety of reasons (i.e., politics, fear of the unknown, etc.). If you want to change her behavior, you may want to take a risk and ask, "If you stay with that vendor, isn't your frustration level just going to get worse?"

The beauty of the TFA approach is its simplicity. Ask and ye shall receive.

Now here are some other questions you can ask to align your thoughts, feelings, and actions better with those of the customer:

1. **Thoughts (Questions to ask your customer.)**

   • How is your company doing overall?

   • When times were better, what were you doing differently?

   • How has your world changed?

   • Do you have enough time to do your job effectively?

2. **Feelings (How is your customer feeling about the situation?)**

   • How do you feel about your workload?

   • How do you feel about the company's future?

   • How do you feel about your own future?

3. **Actions (What is the customer doing to control the situation?)**

   • What are you doing to change things?

   • Is there anything I can do to help the situation?

Do you realize what you've accomplished with these questions? You've uncovered a customer's pain. You've taken your customer out of her comfort zone and made her open up. Most importantly, you've armed yourself with the information necessary to analyze and sell against her pain. Hey, you're a quick learner.

Thoughts, feelings, and actions are three fundamental stages to any sale because each relates to making an emotional connection. For the most part, if you can't make an emotional connection, there won't be any sale. Sorry.

In reality, thoughts, feelings, and actions are essential to closing a sale, or being successful in public relations, shepherding, bricklaying, you name it. How we think, feel, and act will determine everything else.

In a sales situation, it will determine whether a customer buys your product or service. In PR, it will dictate whether a publicist connects with a reporter as well as whether a buyer eventually reacts to a brand. And in life itself, thoughts, feelings, and actions will factor into every decision.

By the way, the bottom line for this particular section is this: If you can verbally validate or confirm for the prospect exactly what her thoughts are, then you can move ahead to uncovering her feelings (i.e., recap what the prospect just told you to reaffirm that you are both on the same page).

Now, let's take an even deeper dive into each of the TFA areas and learn how they impact your sales world.

THOUGHTS: THE KEY TO BUILDING RAPPORT

A salesperson builds rapport by exercising the ability to enter the prospect's world. The best salesperson makes a customer feel as if he completely understands her wants and needs. He creates a strong common bond. In effect, rapport building is the essence of successful communication. Master it, and you master your sales world.

No matter what you want in life, you can get it by building rapport. If you can fill the needs of the people who have what you want, bingo—they'll fill your needs as well. Rapport building works in sales, public relations, and life itself.

Tom Peters' *In Search of Excellence* profiled a number of then-successful companies. (Some have since floundered.) Each shared a few common beliefs. One was treating people with respect and dignity. Each company perceived people as its greatest asset. Each went above and beyond the call of duty to attract and retain the best talent. Each fostered an environment that was both entrepreneurial and collaborative. While it may seem that the two goals are at odds with one another, the fact is they coexist in the best organizations, they enable them to build rapport with their best employees, and vice versa.

Think about how much more energized you'd be if your company rewarded your business development skills while providing a support infrastructure to aid and nourish you throughout the hunting and gathering process. A company we know had a superstar salesperson who felt that he succeeded with little or no support from management. While he was writing the lion's share of his company's business, this guy had to make his own plane and hotel reservations, make copies of his own sales materials, etc. We intervened. We went directly to management and suggested that the star be provided with administrative support (justifying our recommendation with a cost/benefit model).

Freed up to focus solely on prospecting, the star became even more entrepreneurial. Crucially, though, he also became more collaborative and team oriented. In the end, everyone benefited.

Regardless of whether you are being nurtured by your company, you can learn to build a better rapport both within the corporation and with your customer or prospect. Here's how: Reach out to your associate or (better yet) to your prospect, and ask, "How can we do this better?" or "How can we work together to achieve greater results?" Now, we'll grant you that these are awkwardly-worded questions, but you'll find an opportunity in almost every sales meeting to ask a variation on one of the questions. Once you do, you'll be taking that critical first step towards building rapport.

Just imagine how much more successfully an internal project would turn out if you could partner with others to find a solution. The same holds true for a sales situation. If you and the prospect can form a team and collectively solve her pain points, you've entered into a much deeper relationship that can, and should, last for years.

OPEN YOUR MIND

If rapport building were easy, we'd live in one happy, peaceful world. Sadly, there are quite a few folks out there who have no interest in building rapport. Ever. But happily, you're not one of them. You're open to learning new things and becoming a better salesperson. So let's examine rapport building and understand the main reason why most salespeople aren't able to do it. It's pretty simple when you look outside the box. One key reason why rapport building fails is that most salespeople think the prospect has the same agenda as they do. Salespeople often see the world in a certain way, and fail to understand the fact that prospects might be looking at things a bit differently.

To change a prospect's thinking, you have to change the way she looks at the world. The way we think colors the way we behave. And guess what? You can learn to think differently, and most importantly, to get others (i.e., prospects) to think differently as well.

The ability to change a prospect's thinking is most crucial in a sales meeting (assuming that he or she isn't buying what you're selling). If your prospect is perceiving your product or service in a negative light, you have to be able to adjust her perception until it encompasses a more positive view. But first, you have to be willing to open up and surrender your current point of view. And that's the rub. No one likes to change. Most people defend their present modus operandi to the death. Remember those grammar school days when a substitute teacher would come in and try to teach something different or new? Some honor roll or brown nose type would invariably raise his or her hand and say, "But, Mrs. Kenney never did things that way."

We run into this all the time at Peppercom. It's a constant battle for us not to get mired in the way we do things just because "we've always done it that way." Here's a typical example. We had retained Dick Harte after we'd been in business for a year or so. Our billings had skyrocketed from zero to about $2 million, and we were feeling pretty cocky. Dick was brought on board to help us crystallize strategic vision. One of the first things he asked us to do was review our capabilities presentation with him. This is the PowerPoint presentation that we deliver in any first meeting with a prospect. We wanted to attract a larger client and asked Dick to review it from a large-client perspective. We thought it was superb.

Our management team saunters into the conference room one day and starts delivering the presentation to Dick, who was playing the role of a prospective client. After about five minutes, Dick held up both hands and shouted, "Stop!" We all looked at each other. "You're killing me," said the good doctor. "All I'm hearing about is you, you, and you. What about me? What about my needs? When are you going to ask about my pain?"

We resisted. "Dick," we said. "This is the way *every* public relations firm presents. It's standard operating procedure to tell a prospect who you are, what you've done, and what you could do for the prospect." The good doctor scowled (his scowls can kill) and snorted, "Well, your standard operating procedure stinks. You've just lost me as a prospect."

After a little more back and forth, we realized that our view of the world was wrong. We needed to put ourselves into our prospect's world in order to make an emotional connection. We totally overhauled our presentation, and have since been told that it uniquely focuses on prospects' needs.

If you are open to changing, you can learn to adopt an objective view of the way you think and act. You may find that it could be improved (like the Peppercom new business presentation). Or you may find that it needs to be completely overhauled.

You must *force* yourself to be open to new ideas and new ways of thinking. The pace of change today is breathtaking. What worked five years ago, or even last year, may no longer work today or tomorrow. Open your mind, or risk being passed by other, more innovative-thinking salespeople. Rigidity and arrogance should be dropped immediately from your behavior and thinking. Drop them. Now. C'mon, drop them. Good. Now open your mind to a new, better way of thinking about sales.

We believe that in any selling situation, there is usually a newer, better, fresher way of thinking. The present way of thinking is almost never as good or effective as a revised approach. If your current approach or tactics aren't working, change your viewpoint. On the other hand, if it ain't broke, don't fix it. (*Authors' note: In 20/20 hindsight, it was obvious that much of Peppercom's early success was due to a robust economy. Happily, Dick's suggested changes enabled us to sell in a much more sophisticated way and be better prepared when the market downturn hit.*)

So what signs can you look for to ensure that you change course before you lose your prospect? Look for nonverbal clues, which we call "silent signals." For example, going back to the Peppercom presentation to Dick, we should have realized that his folded arms and the fact that he was leaning back in the chair were signs that he was disinterested and bored. If we had known to pick up on those signals, we would have realized that we needed to switch gears immediately and do something differently, on the spot, in order to engage Dick. *(Authors' note: We teach you how to read and react to "silent signals" later in this chapter.)*

The best communicators understand that they have to connect with a prospect. To do so, they may have to change their language, their breathing patterns, or even their gestures until they lock into a formula that aligns with the way the prospect is acting and feeling.

Communication is key to building rapport. If a prospect ends up doing the exact opposite of what you'd hoped for, don't blame her. Blame yourself. You didn't figure out how to get your message through and build rapport. (Bad salesperson. Bad.)

There's a great public relations technique that you can use to connect better with a prospect. We use it all the time in media training. We tell our client executives that whenever and wherever possible, they should personalize the selling message to the reporter or editor. By that, we mean try to get the reporter to envision how the product or service in question could impact her personal life.

Case in point—we were helping to launch a post-9/11 software product that would provide government agencies at the local, state, and federal levels with information and instructions on how to plan and react to biological and chemical terrorist attacks. The software, when wedded to a live Internet connection, could simulate over 100 different types of attacks, and based upon current weather conditions, could tell authorities in what direction they should send local residents to avoid harm. It was a great product, but lots of reporters weren't biting. It seemed too ethereal to them. So we trained our lead spokesperson to personalize the pitch. He went to the *Des Moines Register,* for example, and asked the local reporter where she lived. When she told him that she lived in Ames, Iowa, he plugged in the coordinates and demonstrated what a dirty bomb attack on Ames would be like. He added in the weather conditions on that particular day, ran the program, and "presto chango," the reporter had a *great* local story.

Reporters and prospects are human beings. But like all of us, they stick with their present views of the situation. It's your job as a super salesperson to change that view. Good luck. Let us know how it goes.

FEELINGS: NOTHING MORE THAN FEELINGS

Remember the table from earlier in this chapter? No? Well, here it is again. (See Table 1.1.)

TABLE 1.1

ASSESSING THE PAIN

Situation/Problem to Be Assessed

Our qualitative research showed that the client's sales force was being perceived by the customer as little more than order-takers. Here's how we assessed the thoughts, feelings, and actions of salesperson and customer alike.

Salesperson's Thoughts	*Customer's Thoughts*
1. I'm doing my job.	1. The salesperson is not listening to me.
2. The company has not trained me to be a high-level consultant.	2. No new ideas are presented.
3. I'm too busy.	3. I'm looking bad to my boss.
Salesperson's Feelings	*Customer's Feelings*
Frustration	Frustration
Anger	Anger
Concern	Concern
Fear	Fear
Salesperson's Current Actions/Behavior	*Customer's Current Actions/Behavior*
Doing business as usual	Looking for a new vendor

You can see that the salesperson's and prospect's feelings were identical (frustration, anger, etc.). Yet their thoughts were totally different, weren't they? That's a little strange, no? Well, the reason why their feelings were identical was that the salesperson hadn't done a good job of aligning their thoughts. Hell, let's call a spade a spade. The guy did a terrible job of aligning their thoughts.

Don't even bother moving to the "feelings" part of your sales call if you can't align your thoughts with those of the prospect. (In fact, if you need a refresher, go back to the previous "thoughts" sections.)

How we feel about someone or something is *paramount* to closing a sale. However, there are different types of feelings. (There's a real revelation, huh?) It's absolutely essential that you understand what the different types of feelings are, how to read them, and how to respond to them. As mentioned earlier, we call it reading the "silent signals."

SO WHAT DOES HER FROWN
REALLY MEAN?

Our silent signals approach will provide you with the clues to reading a prospect's nonverbal behavior. And boy, is that ever crucial to a successful sales meeting.

There are so many things to observe in your prospect's unconscious gestures—such as how she responds to your product proposal, or how she reacts to your way of enhancing the pain—and so many ways in which you need to respond in turn that you may ask, "How can I ever keep all these things in mind and still sell my product or service?"

You can. But you'll need practice. For example, when reading your prospect's silent signals, expect to miss a lot at the beginning; stay relaxed, keep your eyes open, and you'll soon see that your powers of observation will start to become second nature, and your own powers of response will grow fearless. But you must practice observing your prospect's silent signals, even where it might feel awkward. One thing is sure: Unless you work it, it won't work.

Oh, and remember, you are not being watched! You are the watcher, the one in control, the one with the broadest view! And you are the one who will get the satisfaction of seeing your thoughts, feelings, and actions create a change in your prospect's attitude and behavior in a positive way. You may even start having fun selling! Just imagine that.

READING THE PROSPECT

Very often, prospects give clues to their feelings through their unconscious gestures in response to something you may say, or to your own body language and tone of voice. In a selling situation, these unconscious clues are usually in response to the amount of tension you create at a meeting. Here is where your powers of observation are crucial since some of the prospect's silent signals will be a clear rejection of what you are proposing. Others will signal a clear acceptance of your proposal. Either way, your ability to read these signs and act on them will differentiate you from your competition.

Here are some signs to look for, how to read them, and some suggested responses. Let's start with the positive nonverbals, or "silent signals," as we call them.

Positive silent signals from a prospect

(These are expressed with various body movements.)

1. Unconscious kiss (see Figure 1.1.)
2. Slight sticking-out of tongue (see Figure 1.2.)
3. Touching lips with forefinger (see Figure 1.3.)
4. Sucking on an object such as a pencil (see Figure 1.4.)
5. Caressing the hair (see Figure 1.5.)
6. Moving an object, such as a pen, toward self (see Figure 1.6.)
7. Inserting a finger in the ear (see Figure 1.7.)
8. Unfolding the arms (see Figure 1.8.)

FIGURE 1.1. Unconscious kiss.

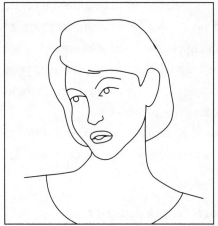

FIGURE 1.2. Slight sticking-out of tongue.

FIGURE 1.3. Touching lips with forefinger.

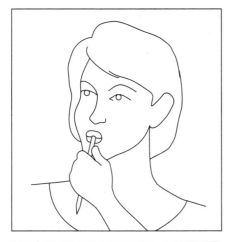

FIGURE 1.4. Sucking on an object such as a pencil.

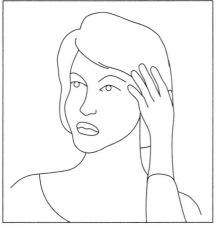

FIGURE 1.5. Caressing the hair.

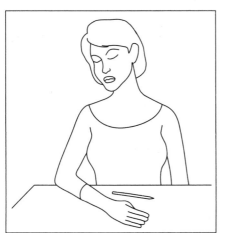

FIGURE 1.6. Moving an object, such as a pen, toward self.

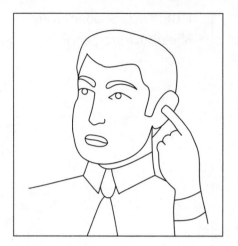

FIGURE 1.7. Inserting a finger in the ear.

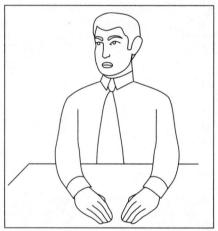

FIGURE 1.8. Unfolding the arms.

It seems like something from the Playboy Channel, doesn't it? Well, relax. These are positive signals. You're connecting with the prospect. So hang in there. Don't get nervous. Don't let up. The prospect is showing you that she or he is accepting what is happening at the meeting.

Negative silent signals

(These are expressed mostly in changes of posture or gestures.)

1. Rubbing the nose horizontally with the index finger (see Figure 1.9.)

2. Moving an object away from self (see Figure 1.10.)

3. Dusting something away from the desk surface (see Figure 1.11.)

4. Clearing the throat (see Figure 1.12.)

5. Crossing the arms (see Figure 1.13.)

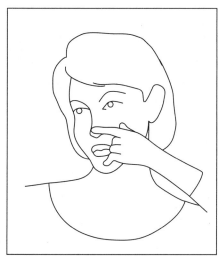

FIGURE 1.9. Rubbing the nose horizontally with the index finger.

FIGURE 1.10. Moving an object away from self.

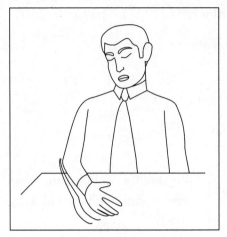

FIGURE 1.11. Dusting something away from the desk surface.

FIGURE 1.12. Clearing the throat.

FIGURE 1.13. Crossing the arms.

Danger, Will Robinson! Danger! Time to change strategies. Be smart and switch gears. Hell, put it in reverse if you see her arms folded. Don't move forward with your proposal. Instead, force yourself to re-establish rapport so that you once again are on the same page as your prospect. You can do this by changing the subject matter of your discussion. For example, if you've been focusing on a specific topic, such as price, and the customer rolls her pen towards you (a negative silent signal), change gears. Perhaps you can segue to your company's value-added services, for example. Or you can change the tone of your voice to become either more or less authoritative.

You can also try a physical response to a customer's negative silent signals, such as:

- Sit back in an open position with your hands clasped behind your head, indicating that you're open to the change.
- Uncross your legs.
- Unfold your arms.
- Lean forward to show real interest.
- Maintain eye contact at all times.

The benefit of reading a prospect's silent signals is that you can adapt and connect with her. Once you know what a person is expressing by her body movements, you'll be able to hone in on the areas where she needs help or where she is suffering pain. It's all part of uncovering and exacerbating pain, which we explain in the next chapter.

The beauty of our approach is that you can practice it all the time: in restaurants, airports, or at the ballpark. Check out how people are interacting with one another, and see if you can identify some of the silent signals we've listed above.

So we've given you the types of questions you need to ask to uncover a prospect's feelings, and we've given you the clues to read a prospect's silent signals. You know you're ready to graduate from phase two when you've confirmed with a prospect exactly what she's feeling. ("So Jane, you're feeling hopeless and overwhelmed and are open to new solutions, correct?")

PUTTING YOUR TFA APPROACH INTO ACTION

You've validated the prospect's feelings. You've fed back to her exactly what her feelings are about the pain she's suffering. You've read her silent signals and perceived positive feedback. Now, my friend, it's time to turn you into Action Jackson. You're ready to do all the things necessary to get this prospect to move forward with a commitment.

To gain a commitment, you need the customer to agree to take some sort of action. The way to do this is to reach out and partner with her to create the action plan together, as a team. Here's how:

- Establish a common goal. What is the prospect's goal(s)? Be very specific.

- Establish the benefits that will arise out of the goal(s).

- Establish the obstacles standing in the way of success.

- Agree upon the action steps necessary to overcome the obstacles.

To sum up the thoughts, feelings, and actions section, let's take a look at how we have used all three to close a sale recently.

A midsized industrial publishing company wanted a novel sales training program to introduce at its national sales meeting. Since we already handled its public relations, we arranged for Dick to meet with the key decision makers in both sales and marketing.

Going into that fateful meeting, we knew these facts:

- The prospect had already met with a traditional sales training company.
- The VP of marketing had been very favorably impressed by them.
- The VPs of sales and marketing would be passing along their recommendations to the company president. All three would decide on a winner.

Dick decided to differentiate our approach clearly from that of the traditional sales training competitor. He wanted to demonstrate how truly out of the box our thinking was, and how it would impact sales quickly by identifying a prospect's pain.

Dick got right to it. (See Table 1.2.) He asked each VP what his pain points were. When he had validated their pain (each was different, by the way), he was able to put them through an assessment by simply asking them their thoughts and feelings about the situation and what they were currently doing about it.

Dick put the prospects through a goal-setting session in which he asked about very specific short- and long-term goals. He also probed benefits and obstacles. He then partnered with them to create an on-the-spot action plan to overcome all obstacles and achieve the goals.

The entire process took less than a half-hour. Both decision makers were totally immersed in our training process without knowing it. Dick finished by asking both VPs if they'd like a sales training program that put their people through the exact same process. When they answered in the affirmative, he asked if they'd be willing to move forward with him.

The VPs were obviously impressed but said that they needed the president's buy-in. As soon as they met with her and took her through the process, she gave a go-ahead. We were hired for the conference and eventually started working with the entire company.

TABLE 1.2

DICK'S TFA APPROACH

Steps	Dick's Actions	Customers' Actions
Step one	Dick asks each customer what's keeping him awake at night.	Cust. 1: Sales are down. Cust. 2: Sales force doesn't know how to sell online products.
Step two	Dick asks TFA questions: • What are your thoughts? • What are your feelings? • What actions are you taking?	Cust. 1: Thoughts—Need to change personnel. Cust. 2: Thoughts—Need training program. Cust. 1: Feelings—Frustrated. Cust. 2: Feelings—Frustrated. Cust. 1: Actions—Creating a new sales process. Cust. 2: Actions—Interviewing training companies.
Step three	Dick probes for specific goals, benefits, and obstacles.	*Goals:* Custs. 1 & 2: Train all managers in new sales process. *Benefits:* Increased sales. *Obstacles:* • Managers' unwillingness to learn. • Budget constraints.
Step four	Dick develops on-the-spot action plan by explaining to both customers that he would train their sales managers using the exact same approach.	VPs agree to recommend Dick to company president.

THE PAIN DOCTOR

To make the messages in our book even more lifelike, we've created a five-act play, *The Pain Doctor*. It stars Johnny Salesman in the lead role and Suzie Customer as the prospect with all that pain. Here's Act One. (Quiet, please.)

ACT ONE

Setting: A cold, wind-swept day. We are in the Spartan offices of Suzie Customer, sales, marketing, and merchandising manager for Big & Large, Inc. She's agreed to meet with Johnny Salesman for 30 minutes. Billy Joel's "Pressure" is playing on Suzie's office boombox.

JOHNNY: Suzie, thanks so much for taking the time to see me today. Pretty nasty out there, isn't it?

SUZIE: *(Arms folded.)* You've got 30 minutes, Johnny. Maybe less.

JOHNNY: *(Notices Suzy's folded arms and how closed down she is. Johnny changes the pace of the meeting and changes the conversation to the music Suzy's listening to.)* OK. Understood. I'm a big Billy Joel fan as well, by the way.

SUZIE: That's nice. What are you here to sell me?

JOHNNY: Actually, I just wanted to ask a few questions. First, how is the company doing?

SUZIE: *(Pushing her pen toward Johnny.)* Don't you do your homework before you call on a customer?

JOHNNY: Oh, sure. I just want to hear your perspective.

SUZIE: Business stinks. Everything stinks. Sales are down. I'm wearing multiple hats, and I have absolutely no time to do anything well. In fact, we're getting fewer incoming calls, and as a result, have fewer opportunities to make a sale. Put that in your pipe and smoke it.

JOHNNY: Actually, I gave up smoking years ago. Evil stuff. Well, let me just go over a few other things. You haven't changed any fundamental sales or marketing strategies. Is that correct?

SUZIE: Dead on, buster.

JOHNNY: OK. Well, what are the main contributors to your sales lag? Do you need to target your prospects better? Are existing customers a source of new business? Do customers understand your unique selling proposition (USP)?

SUZIE: *(Arms folded again.)* Do you always ask so many questions? You must be a blast at a cocktail party. Let me give you some quick answers. It's the economy, stupid. Existing customers aren't opening their wallets, so no, they aren't a source of new business. Yeah, I guess we could do a better job of targeting prospects. And boy, our prospects better understand our USP, or some heads will be rolling in the morning. Does that satisfy you? Are you happy?

JOHNNY: Au contraire. But I do understand. So let me just make sure you and I are in alignment here before moving on . . .*(Johnny proceeds to list Suzie's challenges.)*

(Curtain comes down. The wind howls even louder outside. We hear thunderclaps in the distance.)

So did Johnny do a good job of uncovering the pain, or what? Absolutely. Did he make sure to uncover all of Suzie's pain? Seems like it. Did he read her silent signals and change the tone and direction of his pitch? Yes. Crucially, did he go back and make sure that Suzie confirmed exactly what her pain points were? You bet. But so what? In fact, you're probably saying to yourself, "OK, self, Johnny uncovered some pain. And he validated it. How does he use it to sell?" Not so fast, dear reader. Not so fast. First, you need to understand how to enhance the pain. We call it "pouring salt on the wound." Read on.

CHAPTER SUMMARY

I. Uncovering the pain is the first crucial step in a four-part process that will help you achieve your sales goals. Uncovering the pain means finding out what exactly is keeping your customer or prospect awake at night. How do you find out what your customer's pain is? Ask questions.

   A. What business problems are keeping you up at night?

   E. How are your company's sales? Down? Flat? Up?

   C. Why do you think sales are down? Flat? Up?

   D. How do you feel about your sales being down? Flat? Up?

   E. Do customers understand your company's unique selling proposition?

II. After you uncover the pain, the three remaining steps are:

   A. Analyzing and enhancing the pain (when appropriate).

   B. Providing a solution.

   C. Getting a commitment.

III. Public relations, the art of ensuring that a company's or person's image is favorably presented with all constituent audiences, provides strategies that you can use to develop a positive image with your prospect and help you sell! These techniques require that you do the following:

   A. Differentiate your company from competitors.

   B. Differentiate your products or services.

   C. Differentiate yourself from average salespeople.

   D. Do research on your prospect's company.

   E. Present yourself as a "thought leader."

    F. Find a possible "champion," a third party who can speak on your behalf and offer additional credibility for you and your company.

IV. Aligning your thoughts, feelings, and actions with your prospect's thoughts, feelings, and actions is essential to closing the deal.

  A. Thoughts

    1. You can make a connection by aligning your thoughts with your prospect's, thus establishing rapport. You can do this by asking a question such as "How can we work together to achieve greater results?" This allows the prospect to think of you as a team working together to develop a solution.

    2. Change a prospect's thinking from the way she always did something to a better way. You can do this by uncovering the pain and providing a solution that eases the pain. (See following chapters.)

    3. Be willing to change your viewpoint if your traditional sales tactics aren't working. If you're not establishing rapport with the prospect, change your approach so that you can experience pain from the customer's point of view.

    4. Validate your customer's thoughts by asking, "Am I to understand that the number-one business pain point keeping you awake at night is [fill in specifics from your meeting]." Don't continue the meeting until you've confirmed her pain points.

  B. Feelings

    1. What is your prospect really feeling? How can you read her signals? Nonverbal clues, called "silent

signals," will help you understand how your prospect is reacting to you.

2. Understanding how to read a prospect's positive and negative silent signals will give you the ability to adapt quickly to the prospect's feelings and enhance your chances of making a sale.

C. Actions

1. Get the prospect or customer to agree to take action and make a commitment. You can accomplish this by doing the following:

   a) Establish the goal(s) with the prospect.

   b) Understand the benefits that will come from reaching the goal(s).

   c) Identify the obstacles that are standing in the way.

   d) Agree upon the action steps necessary to overcome these obstacles. This should lead to a commitment by the prospect to take this to the next step.

CHAPTER 2

Enhancing the Pain

(Pouring Salt on the Wound)

Having uncovered a prospect's pain, you must make it clear that you fully understand it. How? By feeding back *exactly* what you've just heard in the prospect's language. Ask for validation. Make sure that you have that validation in your hip pocket before you go for the jugular. For example, after uncovering one prospect executive's pain, we validated it by asking, "It's our understanding that because you've been busy traveling and 'putting out fires,' you've been unable to institute any sort of sales training program and feel like a failure as a result. Is that correct?"

Once you've confirmed that you understand the exact scope and nature of the pain, you need to make it even worse. We know that sounds brutal, but hey, life is brutal. The *only* way to go beyond mere rapport building to close a sale (which is what all those evil, competitive sales books are telling you to do) and actually sell, is to enhance a prospect's pain.

But first, let us pass along a caveat. Enhancing the pain is not for the faint of heart. Shrinking violets need not apply. Enhancing the pain calls for risk. Lots of risk. To enhance the pain, you must be willing to take the chance that you might lose the sale if you agitate the prospect to the point where she ends the meeting and shows you the door. Not to worry, though. We show you how to get right to the brink, and no farther, before reeling in the prospect.

That said, there's sometimes a lot of nuance in a selling situation. Consequently, you need to read when to pour salt on the wound and when to leave things alone. It's often a judgment call. For example, there may be instances where, based upon verbal and silent signal clues, you wouldn't want to exacerbate the pain. You may have established such a good rapport that you can go right to the close. Other times, it may not be worth the risk to pour salt on a wound.

Consider this case in point: One of our client's salespeople had a long-standing relationship with a major customer. Rather than rock the boat by trying to sell in an experimental new project, he opted instead to leave the relationship as is. His rationale: It wasn't worth the risk. A different salesperson with the same company had a small, project-by-project relationship with a deep-pocketed customer. She saw risk-taking as a smart move, so she went ahead and tried to sell the experimental project.

In the final analysis, *you* need to assess whether or not it's worth taking the risk.

VALIDATION

As noted previously, before you can enhance the pain, you must validate it and make sure you're heading down the right path.

For example, your trusty authors were in a recent prospect meeting with a chief executive officer. This woman was dealing with a serious amount of pain. Her company's sales were off by five percent. She told us that she felt *personally* responsible. She was traveling constantly, putting out one fire after another, and had no clear idea how to turn around the bleak sales picture.

In a traditional sales setting, the strategy would call for empathizing with the prospect's pain. Empathy is nice and works well in a Hollywood movie, but this is war. Empathy won't empower the CEO to sign on the dotted line. Why not? Because the traditional sales approach doesn't uncover, validate, and exacerbate the specific pain points causing the prospect's distress. It doesn't prove to the prospect that you understand her pain.

In this particular instance, sales mirrors life. When we see someone in pain, we administer a bandage and try to make nice. In so doing, we are showing that we care about a person. In sales, though, you need to do more than care. You need to demonstrate that you understand the pain and can ease it. To do so, you need to escalate the pain. By escalating the pain, you go far beyond rapport building to establish an intense bond based upon mutual understanding.

Pain-based selling has a much greater impact than empathy-based selling. In fact, empathy in a sales setting is actually apathy. It sounds and looks nice, but the bottom line is that it doesn't solve a customer's problem. No corrective steps are taken when a salesperson shows empathy. You end up patting each other on the back, and the prospect maintains the status quo (or goes looking for someone who can provide a solution).

Our approach calls for risk and provocation because we're risky, provocative guys. Make sense?

Getting back to our case study, we went right after the beleaguered CEO and actually poured salt on her open wound. How? By sharing relevant public relations case studies and sales war stories. Having done our homework and downloaded various articles from the Web, we shared famous (or shall we say infamous) examples of executives who had been in similar situations, had taken no decisive action, and had seen their jobs and their annuities vanish into thin air. We also related war stories from our personal experiences. In each instance, the indecisive executive was eventually kicked upstairs or shown the door. Nasty stuff, huh?

We had taken our prospect *completely* out of her comfort zone. . . in other words, she no longer felt safe and comfortable. We've found that people usually make decisions only when they are taken out of their comfort zones and forced to face an issue, or pain.

What did we do next? After hearing the CEO's problem and analyzing it in the moment, we asked a few fundamental questions (again utilizing the thoughts, feelings, and actions approach discussed in the first chapter).

We asked her what her thoughts were about the current business downturn. We asked if she had changed her overall corporate strategy. When she replied in the negative, we asked what her thoughts were about staying the course. Clearly, we were beginning to exacerbate her pain. Next, we queried her on her feelings, asking how she felt about the current situation. The silence was deafening. Her silent signals (i.e., folded arms, sitting away from us, constantly checking her watch, etc.) threatened death, or worse. She said she felt like a total failure. She believed that she had let the organization down, in general, and the sales force, in particular. For the pain doctors, this was manna from heaven.

While it may seem to you like we had created the pain, we hadn't. It existed well before we set foot in the CEO's conference room. We merely uncovered it and then enhanced it with our stories and our questions. Why? Because *most* sales are made when a prospect has been taken out of her comfort zone.

Here's a quick chart showing different challenges people face in life. (See Table 2.1.) Next to each challenge is a suggested way in which to pour salt on the wound to exacerbate the pain in order to reach a solution. On the far right, you'll see the likely end result.

See if these scenarios don't make sense.

TABLE 2.1

Problem	How to Enhance the Pain	Altered Behavior
Smoking	"Keep this up and you'll die."	Person becomes anxious and seriously considers quitting.
Tardiness	"You're letting your team down."	Person feels guilty and starts taking steps to improve his or her punctuality.
Poor golf scores	"You might be the worst golfer I've ever seen."	Golfer knows he or she needs to take corrective action, and begins practicing.
Talented, but arrogant, executive with a major attitude problem	"You may be good, but the last person who offended everyone got fired."	Executive becomes frightened and realizes it's time for an attitude adjustment.

RISK IS GOOD

Remember the Gordon Gekko character played by Michael Douglas in the movie *Wall Street*? He became famous for his line, "Greed is good." Well, in our case, (and we hope yours as well), we believe that *risk* is good. Salespeople need to take risks in order to connect with a prospect and sell successfully. Risk differentiates you. It also enables you to make that crucial emotional connection in order to sell. And it will empower the prospect to partner with you to cement the deal. We believe that it's fun to take risks and push the envelope. Hey, you only go around once.

In fact, it's risky *not* to take risk. Think about it. If you had gone through that very same meeting we just described and not poured salt on the wound, you wouldn't have made the sale. If you had empathized with the prospect, you both would have had a warm and fuzzy feeling, but there would have been no sense that pain was involved, or that a solution to that pain was needed. And sadly, there would have been no sale. Why? Because sympathetic salespeople don't differentiate themselves. Pain doctors do.

Once you have opened the wound and poured salt on it, you can apply first aid by borrowing from such classic public relations techniques as leveraging proven case studies to underscore how you've successfully solved relevant situations in the past. Remember when we talked about how PR provides third-party credibility? When you have articles or case studies depicting work you've done for others, it does the talking for you, providing powerful credibility in the process. Even better, you can bring along an article *you* have authored that was published in an industry trade magazine. (Imagine how that would differentiate you from the average salesperson! We show you how to write and publish your own article in the final chapter.)

THIRD-PARTY CREDIBILITY

We often succeed in interesting reporters from *The Wall Street Journal* or *The New York Times* in covering our clients' goods or services by leveraging case studies that are real-life stories depicting a customer's cost-benefit ratio. This is just like what we did in the meeting described above. But in dealing with the media, we use third-party case studies to provide proof points that our clients can, in fact, accomplish what they claim.

You, the salesperson, should do the same. When the prospect opens up and shares the pain, be prepared with a second set of case studies. No, not more examples of other executives who are now collecting unemployment checks. Instead, be prepared to discuss or hand out case studies that demonstrate how you've helped other executives through *exactly* the same type of scenario.

Going back to our original CEO story, we uncovered the pain, validated the pain, poured salt on the open wound with examples of people who had failed, and then (drum roll, please), we began to ease the pain. We told her of a company whose sales force had long been successful selling product benefits and low prices. When the economy headed south, however, their sales figures followed suit. The heat was on the company's president to turn things around. We asked for a first meeting. After doing our "pain thing," we recommended a quick, but effective, cure: consultative selling, the four-step process detailed in this book. We developed a program that taught the sales force how to assess and sell against their prospect's pain. The end result was a much more meaningful customer relationship with a higher-level decision maker. The company had metamorphosed from taking one-off orders to forging senior-level customer partnerships. The company turned things around, and the president came out smelling like a rose.

When we were done relating our war story, our CEO's eyes lit up. There was a perceptible change in body language. She leaned forward, moved our proposal towards her, and uncrossed her arms. She realized two things:

1. There was hope for her and her company after all, and

2. We had shown her exactly how we would solve the problem by walking her through our pain process.

In effect, we had used the same formula to sell her that we would subsequently use with her sales force to help them turn things around. In a very subtle but effective way, we had provided our prospect with a sneak peak into our methodology. We had uncovered her pain, analyzed and validated it, further intensified it, and then empowered her with a reason to work with us. When the dust settled, the pain doctors had another customer.

OK, CODY AND HARTE, SHOW US WHAT RISKS *YOU'VE* TAKEN

In order to sell against a customer's pain, you have to be willing to take risks, especially when you get to the point of exacerbating a customer's pain points. We're strong proponents of risk-taking and have, in fact, taken some considerable risks of our own. Here are some examples.

Picture Dr. Richard Harte as a 40-year-old. We know it's difficult, but open your mind a little. The year is 1977. Jimmy Carter is in the White House. John Travolta is disco dancing his way to fame and fortune in *Saturday Night Fever*. And Dick's coauthor is graduating cum laude from Northeastern University.

The middle-aged Dick is at a crossroads in his life. A recent divorcee with two kids, he has been laboring in the printing industry for the past 22 years. (Geez, Dr. Harte, that means *Eisenhower* was in the White House when you started your career!) Anyway, Dick has been absolutely miserable for the past 5 years. He's extremely stressed out and is simply not enjoying life at all. (Who could with all that heinous disco music?) So Dick decides that it's time to make a total break and do something he's always wanted to do: help others.

Walking away from his career meant that Dr. Harte had to sell his ownership in the business form/label company he'd helped build. It was tough, but as soon as he did it, Dick's stress levels dropped faster than President Carter's popularity polls.

So he was free of the high-stress job, but the man still needed to put bread on the table. Plus, Dick wanted to start a brand new career. That meant going back to graduate school, completing the required courses, and writing a dissertation (which was no easy task, as you'll see). So for six long years (that would put him into the first Reagan Administration if you're still keeping score), Dick worked as a sales trainer during the day and pursued his doctorate at night.

To complete the doctoral dissertation, Dick convinced a client, the Motorola Corporation, to let him design a study. He measured sales results in three territories where he had trained the sales force against three territories where he hadn't. The lucky three groups that he'd trained significantly outperformed the others and validated the critical role played by imagination and persistence in the selling process. *(Authors' note: Chapter 5 covers imagination and persistence techniques in depth.)* With his dissertation completed and his theories proven, the good doctor hung out his shingle and went to work in an entirely new field: behavioral psychology and strategic consulting. Today, Dick is a recognized authority in the field whose work and theories have been published in leading trade journals and consumer lifestyle publications.

Now, let's skip ahead to the mid-1990s and Steve's midlife crisis. The year is 1994, and Bubba is holding court in the White House. Our coauthor has just turned 40. *(Authors' note: Wow. Steve and Dick were both 40 years old at the time of their respective crises.)*

Steve was serving as the hand-picked successor to the CEO of a large global advertising agency. It looked like a sweet situation, but it wasn't. The CEO had no desire to turn over the reins, and in fact, did everything possible to thwart our coauthor's success. In fact, Steve found out that he was just the latest in a long series of "hand-picked" successors who just never seemed to measure up. Totally disillusioned, he quit after just 15 months and chose to start his own small firm with a fellow refugee from that same agency.

Risky? You bet. Steve was in his early 40s, with two kids, two cars, and a large mortgage. But as far as he was concerned, the timing was perfect to take a risk. Confident that he could always find a job, Steve had always wondered whether he could make it as an entrepreneur. Rather than wait until it was too late (from an actuarial standpoint, that is), Steve moved ahead. The cost-benefit ratio made sense. Seven years later, Peppercom is recognized as one of the top midsized independent public relations firms in the country, with offices in New York, San Francisco, and London. The firm has won a slew of awards, and represents a "who's who" of Corporate America. And Steve couldn't be happier. (Well, he'd be happier if the Mets won the World Series. But that's beyond his control.)

THE ONLY THING WE HAVE TO FEAR. . . IS FEAR ITSELF

Dick and Steve could have avoided risk by staying put in their previous career paths. Instead, they took chances. And they've both become successful doing exactly what they wanted to do.

The one big obstacle standing in the way of risk-taking is fear. Fear, in turn, creates avoidance behavior. As a result, many of us don't take risks and end up living dull, unfulfilled lives. At the time of his first inaugural address, President Franklin D. Roosevelt said, "The only thing we have to fear is fear itself." Truer words were never spoken.

Let's take a look at what we call "avoidance behavior," and how it relates to fear. Lots of people are mired in their current situations because of it. Fear is linked to behavior, the most common of which is avoidance behavior. It all dates back to our childhoods. Avoidance behavior surfaces when fear triggers a childhood memory.

Remember when we talked about Steve's displeasure with his job at the advertising agency? Well, that was an understatement. He hated it. Despised it. Why? Because it had triggered an earlier memory. You see, that CEO who Steve was reporting to reminded him of his Catholic grammar school principal, Sister Catherine Winifred. Sister Catherine was a Sister of Charity. Talk about a misnomer. This woman was anything but charitable. Corporal punishment and fear tactics were the order of the day. Like many others who went to Catholic schools in the 1950s and 1960s, Steve had some brutal experiences. Anyway, cutting to the recent past and the ad agency job, Steve's CEO reminded him *exactly* of Sister Catherine Winifred (even though the genders were different). This guy was so autocratic and so negative that Steve felt like he was back at St. Francis Grammar School. It got so bad that Steve just shut down. He stopped going to work for several weeks and couldn't even jump on a train because he so feared the confrontation with the CEO. How'd he get past it? By following Dr. Harte's self-encouragement model. (See Chapter 1.) He also created vivid action goals, such as finding a new way to interact with the CEO. As a result, Steve was able to get back into the agency scene and succeed long enough to figure out his next step.

Lots and lots of salespeople practice avoidance behavior. Some general symptoms can include sloppiness in dress or work, chronic absenteeism, drinking, and overeating. In fact, we bet that guy across the aisle from you is practicing some sort of avoidance behavior right now. Is that his third or fourth Dewars on the rocks?

Avoidance behavior manifests itself in sales in different ways:

- fudging or faking sales reports
- submitting phony call reports
- avoiding cold calls
- missing important meetings
- consciously or unconsciously misinterpreting the quality of a sales meeting
- buying our book but never actually reading it

Invariably, this type of avoidance is caused by a childhood trigger. Typically, it was that big test in third or fourth grade that you didn't prepare for and flunked as a result. You failed then, and your mind tells you, you'll fail this time as well. So you fall back on excuses. You didn't make the numbers because you were "too busy." You didn't make the cold calls because of time restrictions. We call this ruse the "I have no time" syndrome (i.e., "Geez Bob, how could I have called on the Vandolay Industries account when you have me loaded up with all of this other stuff," etc.). It's a great excuse. But it's an excuse.

Or how about the following manifestation of avoidance behavior? You can't understand why you didn't get the business. It was a "great" meeting. Everything went swimmingly. But for some bizarre reason, the customer went with a competitor. Sometimes we hear this comment at Peppercom. We'll have a meeting set up with a prospect and the team will come back bubbling over with enthusiasm. "It was a great meeting. We've got this one," they'll say. Yet sometimes we end up not getting the business. Why? Because our people didn't take the time to make sure that their thoughts, feelings, and actions were in alignment with the prospect's. What they thought was a great meeting had, in fact, been a mediocre experience for the prospect.

Gaining alignment is really nothing more than correctly reading a customer's silent signals and restating her verbal pain points. So for example, if a customer says that she's thinking of putting your account up for bid (and keeps her arms folded as she breaks the news), something is obviously wrong. Assuming that you've built some sort of rapport with the customer, you should ask her about her thoughts (i.e., "What's going on? Why is the account up for review?"). This should pinpoint where her unhappiness lies and provide you with an opportunity to forestall her decision.

There's also nothing wrong with identifying her feelings about putting the account in review. This, in turn, will enable you to uncover your own feelings (which are hopefully not too defensive) and pave the way for a discussion about alternative solutions.

Sometimes, salespeople are so anxious to please their management that they overstate the reality of what happened in the meeting. That being said, it's important to note that each situation is unique, and only *you* will know whether or not your thoughts, feelings, and actions were truly in alignment with the prospect's.

Salespeople who practice avoidance behavior tend to confabulate. They make up their own version of the truth. And in the end, they fail.

So how do you overcome this nasty habit? Just like Steve did with his large agency nightmare, you follow our self-encouragement and goal-setting guidelines.

Here's another avoidance behavior story for you to ponder. It comes from the annals of Dr. Harte's psychology practice. One patient, who we'll call Jack Posenreide, was a very successful guitar player who had performed on and off Broadway for years. For whatever reason, though, he had completely lost the ability to play in front of audiences. When the time came, he panicked.

After a complete assessment by the good doctor, Dick found that while Jack loved music, he had not played live in more than 10 years. More to the point, during his last live performance, Jack had actually bolted from the stage while it was rising in front of the audience. Since that incident, Jack had completely avoided picking up his guitar. He even stopped listening to music altogether. The paralysis affected other parts of his life as well. Relationships had soured, and he found himself in a constantly nervous condition.

During his couch time with Dick, Jack confessed that he was terrified to use the elevator in Dr. Harte's building to visit the 26th floor office. On one day, Jack completely panicked when he got near the window in Dick's office. (Actually, if you saw Dr. Harte's office, you'd panic too. It's like something out of an *Austin Powers* movie, with a broken jukebox and furnishings time-warped from back in the 1960s. There's even a stuffed Barracuda lying on his bed.)

Getting back to poor Jack, Dick used regression techniques to uncover incidents from the patient's youth. In so doing, Dick found that when Jack was four years old, his father had asked him to jump from a deck, promising to catch him. Well, the bastard purposely let little Jack fall. Afterwards, he told Jack "never trust anyone in life, not even your own father." Imagine the psychological damage done to the poor little fellow!

The cause and effect of Jack's performance problems were now crystal clear. He suffered from a fear of heights. As a result, Jack panicked anytime he was in a situation where height was involved, such as a performance stage. The last time he had been on stage and the platform began rising, Jack panicked and immediately jumped off, never to return. His career tanked, and the distrust his father had instilled soured his adult relationships.

By openly discussing his fears and following a cognitive behavioral psychology program created by Dick, Jack has been able to become a healthy, functioning individual. He's playing the guitar again and is happily married with two kids. Sadly though, Dr. Harte's office décor has remained time-warped from the 1960s.

FEAR OF THE DARK

Dick Harte has his own story about fear. As a very young child during World War II, Dick remembers being involved in air raid drills. Living in Brooklyn with his mom and dad, Dick recalls black shades on every window being pulled down and lights being turned off whenever an air raid signal would wail. Since his father was working at the nearby Brooklyn Navy Yard, young Dick was alone with his mother. He recalls being terrified of the darkness.

This traumatic childhood event manifested itself years later. In his mid-40s, Dick began suffering from insomnia. There was a long period of time when he got very little sleep at night. As the problem intensified, he found himself doing everything possible to avoid getting into bed at night. Often, he didn't fall asleep until 2:00 or 3:00 a.m. There was a specific four-month period when Dick even suffered severe panic attacks. He eventually sought help and underwent significant therapy in combination with medication to relieve the sleep anxiety. He solved the problem. As a cognitive behavioral psychologist, he now works with people who have some of the same irrational fears as the one that disrupted his own life.

Avoidance behavior can be overcome. You can use self-encouragement techniques to reinforce positive thoughts, feelings, and actions, and to encourage yourself. You can create your own action plan as well. You can communicate with yourself and manage yourself. You can also use your imagination in a very positive way to get yourself out of neutral. We give you the tools necessary to do each.

THE FEAR FACTOR IN SALES

Fear is a major impediment to success. It can manifest itself in many ways. In sales, many salespeople are afraid to lose the sale. So they don't take risks. Here's a case in point. If a customer tells a salesperson that his or her price is too high, the salesperson will report back to management that price was the only hurdle to success. More often than not, price alone isn't the obstacle. In the same setting, a creative, risk-taking salesperson will counter the price objection with product benefits, or perhaps added values that would translate into savings. All it takes is a little intestinal fortitude.

Here's a personal example of a little risk-taking in a public relations setting. We had reached the final round for the account of a *Fortune* 1000 multinational manufacturing company. We were competing against the incumbent, which happened to be one of the largest public relations firms in the world. So we had our work cut out for us.

In preparing for the final presentation, we had conducted extensive research into the prospect firm. Our findings showed that the company had received little, if any, publicity in the major business press. We wanted to demonstrate this lack of awareness by projecting a slide in the presentation that read, "Company ABC: One of Corporate America's best-kept secrets." We wanted to introduce the slide by saying, "If *The Wall Street Journal* wrote an article about your company today, this might be the headline." Our very next slide contained another headline that we hoped would appear in the *Journal* after we had been working on the account for several months. Naturally, the second headline was much more positive and heralded the company's key positioning and message points.

This strategy was high-risk. In effect, it would indict the current vice president of marketing by implying that his regime hadn't generated sufficient awareness of the company. We agonized over whether or not to show the slide. It was true, and we did feel uniquely qualified to turn the situation around. But it was also provocative enough to anger the prospect and possibly cost us the account. What to do? We sought out the VP's subordinate, who was our champion in the pitch. (We discuss the importance of champions in a later chapter.) This champion would also be in the final presentation and knew the VP extremely well. Unfortunately, he wasn't sure how the VP would react and left it up to us to make the decision.

We opted to leave the slide in. However, we worked out a subtle strategy to go along with the slide. Rather than just showing the slide without commentary, we instead decided to ask the VP if he agreed that the company hadn't received much business publicity up to this point. He agreed. Then we asked, if that was in fact the case, whether or not this next slide would be an accurate portrayal of a *Journal* headline. He agreed that it would. In fact, he got totally charged up by the conversation and began editing the headline on the spot. When he was done, we, "as a team," had created a desired headline that we would try to make appear in print. By taking the risk of showing the potentially offensive headline, we had demonstrated our concern and understanding and won the VP over in the process. About a week later, we were awarded the account.

ON THE ROCKS

We couldn't end this chapter on risk-taking without talking about our "on the rocks" philosophy.

We all know people who blame others for their problems. In fact, you could say that our entire society embraces this philosophy. Just watch the nightly news some time and see if the latest court case doesn't feature a defendant who blames everyone else for the crime he or she committed. Anyway, these individuals play the role of "victim" throughout their lives.

Conversely, there are people who are always seeking to improve their lots in life. They take courses. They seek new opportunities. They take chances. Hey, you're one of those people. Just by picking up this book, you've demonstrated a desire to learn something new. You've opened yourself up to new thoughts, concepts and ideas that will improve your daily life and make you a better salesperson. There, have we made you feel a little bit better? Good.

Now, let's go back to those bad guys—the ones who blame others for their problems, the ones who hang out "on the rocks." They're victims and see themselves as being in exactly the same situation as shipwreck survivors who cling to the rocks, paralyzed with fear, desperately scanning the horizon for rescue. They never make waves. They tend to be dull, boring, and uninteresting. They're usually not happy but often pretend to be. Sounds like a few politicians we all know, doesn't it? These folks could be rich or poor. It doesn't matter.

A certain percentage of people (you and we, just to name three) get off the rocks and become the "source" for everything they do. We understand the purpose in our lives.

Our purpose in life must be vivid and lifelike to us. Many people verbalize their purposes in life with superlatives ("I want to be the very best husband," or "I want my family to be happy."). While these are noble sentiments, they are not vivid or lifelike enough in and of themselves. For example, how do you act on "being the best husband?" What do you do to fulfill that goal? Specifics need to be added. Otherwise, you'll end up as a husband on the rocks with a marriage on the rocks.

Let's suppose that your purpose in life is to enjoy yourself. You want to enjoy yourself in every situation, whether it's work or play. Once you've defined your purpose and it's vivid in your imagination, you need to do something to make it actually happen. You must take risks.

Here's a specific example. A friend of ours is deeply ensconced in middle age. He's bright, articulate, and successful. But for a variety of personal reasons, he yearns for a brand new type of challenge. So he decided to run a marathon. If you looked at this guy, marathon running would not be the first thing to pop into your mind.

To his credit though, this executive set specific benchmarked goals to prepare him to compete in the marathon. He started slowly, running 2 or 3 miles every other day. After a few weeks, he increased the mileage to 5 miles a day. One day a week he ran a longer route. Within three months, this Frank Shorter wanna-be was running 10 miles a day and 20 miles on Saturdays.

He dropped weight, gained energy (or so he claims), and eventually ran a marathon in under four hours. To this day, he credits the specific benchmarked running program as the reason for his success.

ENJOY YOURSELF

You have to take risks to be happy in life. Sound bizarre? Not really. Just about everyone's goal is to enjoy life, right? But suppose you're stuck in a dreary job. What then? That's not enjoyable, and there's nothing you can do about it, right? Wrong. You have to be willing to take a risk and leave the job to find one that is more satisfying. If your personal relationship isn't working, you need to risk walking out on it in order to find happiness. If the stock market is making you unhappy (or worse), take a risk by diversifying your portfolio. *(Authors' note: We are not qualified financial advisers. If you lose your shirt, don't come after us.)*

Countless people just can't bring themselves to get off the rocks. They get stuck and accept their misery. And so they live dull, uninteresting, and unrewarding lives. It's pretty awful when you think about it, isn't it?

Many salespeople are stuck on the rocks. They're afraid to take a chance and ask tough questions. Most likely, they'd be afraid to learn the thoughts, feelings and actions methodology we suggest in this book. Unquestionably, they'd be fearful of uncovering a prospect's pain and pouring salt on the wound. But hey, you're not one of those dolts. You *are* open to new ideas and new approaches. You *are* open to mastering the four steps.

If you're willing to get off the rocks, you'll find yourself earning lots of money and dealing with customers who are interested in your products and services. Of equal importance, you won't waste time with people or prospects who are only interested in wasting your time because they have nothing better to do.

What's the bottom line if you *are* able to get off the rocks? That's easy. You'll be a *much* happier person. And hey, wasn't that your goal in the first place?

THE PAIN DOCTOR—

ACT TWO

Setting: Suzie Customer and Johnny Salesman have left Suzie's office and are now strolling towards Big & Large's company cafeteria. Suzie has a major headache and needs a third cup of coffee to wash down some Tylenol Sinus capsules. We can hear thunder pealing in the distance. The rain is bouncing off the cafeteria windows. Huey Lewis's "The Heat is On" is playing on the sound system. The curtain rises and the lights go down. You there in the front row, stop fidgeting in your seat!

SUZIE: I hate these sinus headaches. It wasn't bad enough that I had to deal with Smudnoff this morning telling me he couldn't close that big account, and as a result, my monthly sales numbers will be even bleaker. Now it feels like that thunder is actually going off inside my head.

JOHNNY: Bummer. I know just how you feel. *(Note to reader: Notice how Johnny starts with empathy and then quickly transforms the empathy into exacerbating the pain.)* My mom suffered from sinus headaches for years. By the way, I want to make sure I understand exactly what is happening in the company and with you personally. Mind if I play it back for you?

SUZIE: Knock yourself out. Oh, miss? I'll take an extra large café latte. You know Johnny, the one good thing about this cafeteria is the café latte machine. So go ahead. . .

JOHNNY: Right. Regular coffee for me, miss. Anyway, the company's sales are way down. You are totally overwhelmed and are now responsible for three separate divisions. There's all sorts of pressure on you to turn the sales thing around, but you're too busy putting out fires. Is that about it?

SUZIE: You forgot the part about my feeling like a total failure.

JOHNNY: Oh, yeah. Right. You feel like a total failure. Hey, didn't you also feel like you were about to lose your job?

SUZIE: . . . The memory of an elephant.

JOHNNY: Well Suzie, I don't want that sinus headache to get any worse, but I've known some other Suzies in my day.

SUZIE: Pray tell.

JOHNNY: Yup. Just like you, they felt totally powerless to change the situation. And worse, they didn't understand the role that consultative selling can play in turning around a sales situation. So as a result, they didn't make any changes in their sales strategies.

SUZIE: And?

(We hear a loud crash of thunder.)

JOHNNY: Oh. They were each fired and replaced with someone else.

SUZIE: There *has* to be another Tylenol Sinus in my purse. I know I put six in here this morning. Anyway, great story, Johnny. Just a phenomenal story. They all got canned? You're making me feel like a million bucks, Johnny, a million bucks.

JOHNNY: Wait. There's more.

SUZIE: My head can't take any more.

JOHNNY: Yeah, but Suzie, you didn't let me tell you about Cecil.

SUZIE: Cecil?

JOHNNY: Cecil Cooper. Ran the sales force in a company very similar to Big & Large. Had lots of the same problems as you. Didn't have sinus headaches though. Cecil was a nose bleeder. Man, could that schnozola bleed when the heat was on. Anyway, I listened to Cecil's pain. Told him about some of the same people I just told you about. Sure enough, his nose opened up and began to bleed. But when I told him about some of the other Cecils we had helped and how we had helped them, he began to feel a lot better. Nose stopped bleeding as well. Cecil hired us. We built in a beautiful consultative selling program for his sales force. And guess what? His sales force was able to open doors that had been closed because they weren't relying on the same old tactics like price anymore. They learned how to probe for their prospects' pain, how to enhance that pain, and then how to ease the pain with his company's services. Cecil got a big promotion and now he's running all of North American sales.

SUZIE: *(Sucking on her coffee stirrer.)* Johnny, you're a nice guy and all. But frankly, this sounds a little too good to be true. And my daddy always told me if something is too good to be true, it usually is. I'm going to need a lot more concrete specifics before moving ahead. And besides, I really don't care about Cecil's story. Our situation is very complicated, and I don't see how you can help us.

JOHNNY: Complicated situations can be broken down into manageable compartments that can be addressed and solved one by one. Actually, that's one of our core differentiators: turning complicated problems into manageable situations. (*Authors' note: Notice how Johnny worked in his company's positioning here.*)

SUZIE: Look, Johnny . . . we don't have a budget . . . period. My sales numbers are down, our entire company is in the toilet right now, and the last thing my boss, Mr. Blimpbinder, is going to want to hear from me is that we need to spend more money to make money. You're wasting your time.

JOHNNY: But if I could show you tangible value that will make you look good to your boss, wouldn't that be worth a few minutes more of your time?

SUZIE: I guess.

JOHNNY: Fine. Can I get you another café latte and a couple more Tylenols?

SUZIE: Why not?

(*The curtain comes down. The wind is still howling, but not quite as badly. The rain seems to have trailed off to a steady drizzle. Did you notice that our man Johnny did a great job of validating Suzie's pain? He went a step further, though, didn't he? He took a risk by letting Suzie know that if she didn't do something to fix the pain, she'd lose her job. He used proven public relations techniques to share case studies of other executives who had "stayed on the rocks" and not made changes. Then, he told his Cecil Cooper case study to ease her pain. Suzie still has her headache, to be sure. And she's practicing some avoidance techniques by telling Johnny his solution sounds too good to be true. But maybe, just maybe, there's a rainbow waiting for her at the end of this particular storm.*)

Some other notes of interest:

Did you notice how Johnny was able to build rapport with Suzie? He empathized, to be sure, but he went beyond empathy. He followed our line of questioning and uncovered Suzie's thoughts, feelings, and actions.

As we move forward, you'll see how Johnny prequalifies Suzie. He'll determine whether she has real interest to solve the pain. And he'll do it quickly.

Johnny's also a master of time management. He'll conclude the meeting in 20–25 minutes. *(Authors' note: Later on in the book, we explain why your meetings shouldn't run longer than 20 to 25 minutes, as well as how to dissect a successful 20-minute sales meeting.)* After 20 minutes, Johnny will know if Suzie is serious and if she is, Johnny will either close her on the spot or hone everything he needs to come back with a final proposal.

And because he's an astute time manager, Johnny will be able to meet with several other prospects on this rainy day.

CHAPTER SUMMARY

I. After you uncover the pain, make sure that you understand it. Repeat it back to the prospect in her own words, and ask for validation. For example, if you had asked the prospect what's keeping her up at night, you may want to say, "So am I to understand that what is keeping you up at night is XYZ?" Make sure that you and the prospect are in total agreement *about* the pain before you move forward to *enhance* the pain. Then, and only then, are you ready to enhance the pain. How do you exacerbate the pain? Ask painful questions and/or relay similar stories to the prospect's situation.

A. If you don't sell more widgets, will your job be on the line?

B. Are you letting down your boss?

C. I knew a VP in your exact situation. She had the same problems with her company and was then fired.

II. Enhancing the pain involves risk and is not appropriate for every situation. Enhancing the pain can lead to closing the sale, but it can also lead to losing the sale. Deciding whether or not to take the risk depends upon the following:

A. The prospect's verbal and silent signals. Read your prospect so you understand how she is feeling.

B. Your level of rapport with the prospect. If you have a strong rapport with the prospect, you may feel more comfortable in taking risks.

C. If you have nothing or very little to lose, and a lot to gain, then pour salt on the wound.

III. Once you enhance the pain, use the public relations technique of providing third-party credibility, having others do the "talking about you" for you. You can accomplish this by doing the following:

A. Showing the prospect published articles or case studies that demonstrate what you or your company has done for other clients.

B. Showing the prospect a bylined article you have written that was published in a trade magazine.

C. Verbally explain the case studies if you don't have a printed copy.

CHAPTER 3

Selling Against the Pain

(Applying Salve to the Wound)

Remember Robin Williams's professorial character in "The Dead Poet's Society?" The teacher who constantly challenged his students to seize the day? "Carpe diem!" he would shout, encouraging them to take advantage of the opportunities that life presented.

Well, guess what? We're encouraging you to do the very same thing. If you've been following our little selling scenario, then you know that there is now an opportunity to seize the moment. Carpe occasio, dear reader. Carpe occasio!

But here's the beauty of our approach; we are *not* suggesting you go for the close at this point. Most sales traditionalists will shudder at our unconventional suggestion. But bear with us. In fact, let's do a quick recap of where we're at in the sales call.

So far, we've asked you to:

- Determine your own pain points before you attempt to uncover your customer's.
- Uncover your customer's pain by asking a series of probing questions.
- Validate that you completely understand the customer's pain before moving forward.
- Make sure your thoughts, feelings, and actions are in alignment with those of the customer.
- If the situation presents itself, enhance the customer's pain.

So instead of going for the close at this point, you should be doing exactly the opposite. The astute salesperson will be seizing this particular moment in the sales meeting to *empower the prospect to move forward*!

"Balderdash," some of you traditionalists may be thinking.

"Pshaw," other readers may be sighing.

"Say what?" you're probably thinking to yourself.

Before you toss the book in the garbage, let us explain.

The prospect may or may not know it, but she's looking for help. In fact, she may be desperately seeking help. But consciously or unconsciously, she wants to know that the vendor she partners with understands her pain and can provide a tailored solution to ease it.

PAIN-BASED
QUESTIONING (PBQ)

So how do we get the prospect to make the decision for us? Ah, here's where that money you shelled out for the book really starts to pay off. We employ *pain-based questioning,* or *PBQ,* our proprietary, gold-plated, cross-examining, put-the-prospect-in-the-driver's-seat methodology.

Here's how it works. *Pain-based questioning* is, in effect, a way in which to elicit new thoughts, feelings, and actions from our prospect. Prospects must think that our service will add value to their businesses. They must feel positive and optimistic about the potential of our solutions, and they must translate those thoughts and feelings into actions by deciding to purchase our services.

Questions get a prospect thinking in different ways. Consider this dialogue in which our questions propose distinctions and lay the groundwork for the prospect to envision different options.

Cody/Harte: How would you describe your company's sales performance year-to-date?

Prospect: It's certainly not very good right now. We get fewer incoming calls and fewer opportunities to make a sale.

Cody/Harte: Well, what are you doing *differently* from the days when your sales were stronger? How are you following through with the sales leads that are coming in? What have the results been?

By asking the questions that we did, we've opened a door to a discussion about what else the prospect could be doing and how we might play a role.

If done in a logical, sequential manner, questions can lead to constructive solutions. Rather than focus on one major problem that limits you to one major solution, the salesperson should instead ask a series of questions designed to probe and uncover multiple solutions and options. The more solutions and options, the more likely it is that you'll find an ideal opportunity for your company's product or service.

So if a prospect says, "My problem is that 9/11 ruined my business, and it hasn't recovered since," we would respond by asking the following:

1. Why do you think that's so?
2. What are your thoughts about the business decline?
3. How do you feel about it?
4. What are you currently doing about it?
5. If I could solve one sales or marketing problem that you are facing right now, what would it be?

Here are some other follow-up questions that we could ask to continue uncovering the prospect's pain points:

1. What are the main factors in your sales decline?
2. If fewer incoming calls are such an issue, will it help to increase the quality of outgoing calls?
3. Do you think that you need to do a better job of targeting prospects?
4. How do you target prospects now?
5. Is this working well for you?
6. Do you think you might also find new business with existing customers?

7. Do you think your customers and prospects understand the full scope of what you offer?

Questions not only uncover pain; they empower a prospect to make a decision. No one likes being forced into a corner, especially a prospect. Prospects are much more likely to feel positive about investing in your company's products or services if they perceive the decision to do so as being entirely their own. Your job as a crack salesperson is to ask questions that make it seem natural and logical for the prospect to say "yes."

So rather than telling a prospect "Hey, we have some great solutions to boost your sales," you might instead ask a simple question. "If I could show you a way to open up doors in companies you haven't been able to pursue before, and give you specifics about the opportunities that exist in each company, would that be of interest to you?" See how much more powerful that is? We're asking the prospect whether she needs something we can provide. It provides the prospect with options and enables her to feel like she's in the driver's seat. Those types of questions enable you to probe the customer's needs more deeply. They elicit a different type of response. They demonstrate that you're reaching out to partner with her.

Questions build needs. It goes without saying that you won't close a sale if the prospect doesn't clearly see the need for your product or service. So you have to build needs during a sales call. Building needs is essential in public relations as well. We use a similar technique to garner a reporter's interest in a client's products or services. Just calling the reporter and saying, "We'd like you to interview company XYZ," is not going to get our foot in the door with the reporter or an interview with our client. However, if we call the reporter and say, "Did you know that X is a real problem in this industry?" and "Do you agree that your readers would be interested in learning about a solution to this issue?" and "Well, company Y has a solution that does this, this, and that," the reporter will listen.

Pain-based questions complement our TFA approach. They typically begin with very pointed phrases, such as, "Is it safe to say..." or "So are you telling me..." or "Have you ever thought..." More fully formed pain-based questions would include:

- "Is it safe to say that your sales force isn't consistent in the messages they send?"

- "So are you telling me that your current program isn't measurable?"

- "Have you ever thought of implementing a sales training program?"

Pain-based questions provide you with an opportunity to connect emotionally with the customer. In fact, the whole premise of pain-based questioning hinges on uncovering a human being's discomfort, and not the vague year-to-date performance of a monolithic corporate structure.

Questions can create needs and convince buyers that they *must* have what you're offering. In effect, questions can empower the prospect to close the sale for you.

Here are a couple of other questions you could use at this point in the sales call:

1. What's the one business issue that keeps you up at night? What do you need in order to solve that issue?

2. What other business problems do you typically take home with you?

The answers to these specific questions will prompt solutions in your mind and will enable you to align yourself with the customer.

So getting back to the bedraggled female CEO we've been spotlighting in the text, we asked her some of these questions:

- What type of training do you currently have in place to solve your sales problems?

- Do you have a full-time sales trainer? If so, what are his roles and responsibilities? If not, why not?
- Is the training program an ongoing process, or a one-off Band Aid?
- Is your sales training being supplemented by other programs?
- In the sales setting, how do you differentiate your company?
- Do you know if your sales force is using that messaging in its selling?
- How are your salespeople differentiating themselves from competitors' salespeople? Have you seen them practice this?
- What key messages do *you* use in selling your company's services?
- Are you confident that the sales force is using the same messages? If they aren't, is there a possibility that you could be confusing the prospect?
- Do we ask a lot of questions, or what?

These questions will work whether your firm is selling high-end consultative services or $1.99 widgets. You'll just have to be creative. Ask questions. Listen to the answers. Typically, the answers will clue you in to areas of opportunity to be seized. Pain-based questioning will also empower the prospect to partner with you. Why? Because the questions you ask will make the prospect think about areas that aren't being addressed; areas where you and your firm can provide solutions.

PERSONALIZING PAIN-BASED QUESTIONING

Many sophisticated politicians and corporate executives make subtle use of pain-based questioning in their speeches and interviews. How many times have you heard a politician ask his or her audience a question about the incumbent's less-than-spectacular record? What do you think they're doing? It's simple. They're empowering the voters to make a decision. And if you follow our strategy, you'll be doing the same thing with pain-based questioning.

But some politicians and executives go a step further. *(Authors' note: Unfortunately, some of them go way too far. But that's another subject for another book.)* They personalize pain-based questioning. When asked to explain a sophisticated campaign platform or cutting-edge product, savvy pols and execs often turn the tables and transform the interviewer into the interviewee.

They do this by asking personalized questions. Case in point: Let's assume an office products executive is being interviewed on CNBC about a new ergonomically designed office chair. When asked about the chair, he turns the interview around by asking the reporter how many hours he or she sits in an office chair. He goes on to ask about his or her lower back pain problems. Or the lower back pain problems of the reporter's fellow journalists. He shares industry research pointing out that lower back pain is the second leading cause of worker absenteeism. *(Authors' note: The common cold is the number-one cause of worker absenteeism.)*[1] Then, he "bridges" to the need for his company's new chair. (See the next section for more details on bridging.)

He's personalized his pain-based questioning skills and empowered the reporter's audience to buy his product. This executive has also used what we call the "problem-solution" method. In this case, the problem is lower back pain, and the solution is his company's chair.

Let's take this a step further and delve into how a salesperson might use pain-based questioning in an actual sales meeting. Let's pretend you're an office products sales representative whose charge is to sell a new, low-end competitor to the Palm Pilot.

We've created the script that follows to dramatize this hypothetical pain-based questioning pitch.

Jack: Jill, I appreciate your time today. I can only imagine how harried your schedule must be since last week's downsizing.

Jill: You have no idea. I lost two salespeople and my administrative assistant. Now they're talking about eliminating corporate communications entirely, so there goes my marketing support materials as well. Management says it wants to grow, but then they cut the resources you need to grow.

Jack: I hear you. It's an old axiom but a true one: You can't grow a shrinking company.

Jill: Amen.

Jack: Anyway, you're busy and I assume your budgets are limited.

Jill: Microscopic would be more like it.

Jack: Got it. Do you own a Palm Pilot now?

Jill: The entire sales force has them.

Jack: Well before I ask how you like them, I wondered if we could enter your schedule next week into our new Wonder Child organizer.

Jill: Help yourself.

Jack: OK. (*Loads data.*) Now, let me show you how the Wonder Child performs three brand new functions that the Palm doesn't. All three will save you enormous time. (*Authors' note: Jack has already established that time is Jill's major pain point.*)

Jill: Wow.

Jack: If you had these three additional components on your current product, how much time would you save each week?

Jill: At least an hour or two.

Jack: Let's say it saves an hour. That's four hours a month, or 48 hours a year. That's two completely free days. Imagine what someone like you, who has absolutely no time, could do with two additional days. Now what if we extended this to your entire sales team? If I could show you how your whole sales force could free up two days each by using the Wonder Child, would you be more willing to move forward with me?

Regardless of whether Jack is able to close the sale with Jill at this point or will have to come back with a detailed proposal, the point is he transformed an ordinary pitch that is usually based on price into one that is personalized and relevant to Jill's world.

BRIDGING AS A TECHNIQUE

Public relations skills can make a huge difference in the selling game. We train our clients to anticipate every conceivable question they might be asked in a media interview. Then, we role-play with them to teach them how best to answer those questions. You'd be surprised how many negative or irrelevant questions are asked during the typical media interview. How does a top politician or corporate chieftain *control* an interview, keep it on track, and deliver the message points most beneficial to his campaign or company? How can you use those same techniques in pain-based questioning?

Actually, one controls an interview by being mindful of communicating key messages at the beginning and end of each meeting. If a negative or irrelevant question is asked, the savvy executive will bridge away from the problem question and get back to the messages that he or she needs to communicate. For example, let's say our CEO is on a local business program and is asked a question about the company's poor stock performance. Rather than getting caught in an area that can't turn out too well, our executive could bridge by responding, "Clearly the stock hasn't performed well in the past few months. But few stocks have. What we're really enthusiastic about is the next-generation widget I'm here to talk about today."

Voila. Our executive has escaped a no-win situation and bridged back to his message.

So how does this same technique work in sales? Let's say you're a newly-hired salesperson who's taking over a large account. You walk into your first meeting and encounter an immediate bridging opportunity (or a potential disaster, depending on your point of view).

Customer: So you're my new rep?

You: That's right. It's a pleasure, sir.

Customer: I wish the pleasure was mutual, but frankly, your company's delivery problems are causing major agita. You know what that is?

You: Yes, sir.

Customer: My neck's on the line, and I'm stuck with a rookie salesperson. My stomach's churning even more.

You: On the contrary,[2] I'm anything but a rookie. First, let me share my background credentials. Second, let me show you how we can work together to turn around the delivery issues and ease your agita.

BECOMING A THOUGHT LEADER

Another way to control a sales meeting is to have total command of facts and figures. In the office products media interview, our intrepid spokesman knew all about lower back pain and its impact on American productivity. He came across as a *thought leader*. And you can too. It's all about research. Do your homework about industry issues. Do a deep dive into the prospect company. Then, when the opportunity presents itself, augment your pain-based questioning with deep industry and prospect company facts and figures. So how do you become a thought leader? It's really not hard, if you're willing to invest the time and effort.

Let's see how our office products executive became a thought leader. He made sure that he knew everything there was to know about lower back pain and its impact on productivity. How? The Web. It's a handy-dandy tool that gives you the brain dump you need.

Our office products guy went to the OSHA site. He visited the HEW site. He visited various workers' compensation and benefits sites (such as *www.SHRM.org*). When he was done, guess who was a thought leader on the subject?

You can take thought leadership to the next level by writing an article about it for a local business publication or vertical industry magazine serving your customer's particular field (i.e., *Chemical Week,* the bible of the chemical industry). Imagine how a reprinted article carrying your name would differentiate you. It would create great credibility for you. Your prospect or client is much more likely to perceive you as a thought leader if you can bring along some published materials. Even better, they'll perceive you as an expert, someone they'd not only feel comfortable partnering with, but someone they'd speak about to others in a positive tone (i.e., "We've just hired The Slickum Company. Their sales guy, Zeke Moed, has written some really cool articles on supply chain issues in our industry. I'll send you a copy," etc.).

You could even take thought leadership a step further and write a book. Just don't try to compete with us.

LISTENING SKILLS

Good salespeople aren't just thought leaders, they're excellent listeners too. Listening provides clarity. The questions we have armed you with will elicit everything you need in order to sell. But remember, never answer your own question. If a prospect's answer is not clear, ask again. If you don't, you'll never align yourself fully with the prospect. No alignment means no sale.

Listening is also critical to making an emotional connection. Voice, tonality, and inflection are all valuable clues as to how a sales call is going. The same is true for a telemarketer who should be listening to the responses from a prospect.

Here's how to listen:

1. Keep quiet and let the prospect talk.

2. Never interrupt. Wait until the prospect has completed his or her thought.

3. As you listen to the problem, begin visualizing how you can address various issues with specific remedies from your past.

4. Allow the prospect to explain to you how your company's products or services could help solve a problem.

5. Repeat what's been said to you so you can validate its accuracy and show the prospect that you've understood what's been communicated. That's a critical part of listening.

In the next chapter, you see exactly how personalizing pain-based questioning, controlling the meeting, and demonstrating thought leadership will enable you to gain a commitment from the prospect. Commitment will lead to the sale, which is, after all, the Holy Grail we all seek.

THE PAIN DOCTOR—

ACT THREE

Setting: We're back in Suzie's office. She has gulped down her café latte and is catching up on her voice mail while Johnny chews the edges of his Styrofoam coffee cup. The wind is still howling, interrupted only by an occasional clap of thunder. Don Henley's "In a New York Minute" is now playing on Suzie's office boombox. The curtain rises. Hey, reader! Turn off your cell phone during the performance. We don't want any interruption.

SUZIE: *(Placing her phone back in its cradle and crossing her legs.)* Damn. Smudnoff says Wire & Hire is delaying its decision to move ahead with us for at least three to four weeks. He promised me they were ready to sign. Now there's a delay until they finalize a contract with some institute or something. Damn. I had that sale factored into this month's numbers as well.

JOHNNY: That's brutal. Had you factored a no-go into your scenario planning?

SUZIE: We did some scenario planning, but to be frank, we really needed Wire & Hire's business.

JOHNNY: Well, I appreciate the predicament you're in. I just need to ask a few more questions about your training so I can provide a solution.

SUZIE: Look, now is not the time. Didn't you hear what I just said? We lost a major piece of business. I don't want to talk about your friggin' training programs.

JOHNNY: Hold it, Suzie. You've just a lost major sale because something went wrong. Maybe it was out of your control. But maybe you could have won that sale. Isn't now *exactly* the time to speak about the kind of training your team needs to convert more calls?

SUZIE: We need sales numbers. Not training programs.

JOHNNY: Can't get one without the other. Proven fact.

SUZIE: Says who?

JOHNNY: *(Pulls out articles demonstrating the value of training.)* By the way, that last clipping you're looking at is from *Sales & Marketing Management* and was authored by yours truly.

SUZIE: Gee. Can I have your autograph? OK, fine, whatever. So training works. Big deal. It takes forever before you see results.

JOHNNY: No it doesn't Suzie. Let me ask about your company's training. What formalized training is in place to help your people sell?

SUZIE: *(Rolls her neck.)* Have you been listening to anything I've been saying? God, my head hurts. With the budget cuts last fall, there hasn't been a budget for training. So if you're selling me a training program, forget it.

JOHNNY: Well, how do you know Smudnoff is selling in the proper way?

SUZIE: He's a trooper. He's come through in the past, and he'll come through again. He has to.

JOHNNY: But hasn't everything changed since Smudnoff was last successful?

SUZIE: *(Leans back in her chair away from Johnny.)* Absolutely not. We still make the very best products in our space. And we're price competitive with every competitor. Our service is second to none.

JOHNNY: *(Leans forward in his chair toward Suzie so he maintains the same distance between them.)* Right. Your company may not have changed. But you, yourself, told me the economy *has* changed. Budgets have been cut, and the widgets that you used to sell by the bucket are now sitting in warehouses collecting dust. In fact, according to industry statistics, sales in your particular space are down across-the-board by seven percent. Everyone is failing. But failure for others can provide opportunity for you. Suppose your salespeople become creative while their competitors continue to run in place. But I forgot. You said that Smudnoff and the others aren't getting any training. So since they're not getting any new training, how will Smudnoff know *how* to sell in this new environment? In fact, if you think about it, wouldn't his learning new skills and approaches enable Smudnoff to uncover how your prospect's world has changed and how to sell against his or her new pain points?

SUZIE: Yeah. I guess so. But it's not that easy.

JOHNNY: Maybe not. But what if Smudnoff changes his ways, learns new skills, and begins to sell, what happens to the sales picture?

SUZIE: Duh. It improves.

JOHNNY: Right. And what happens to your life?

SUZIE: *(Showing just a trace of a smile.)* It sounds like it gets easier. But I'm still not convinced that this will work in my case.

(The curtain comes down.)

So did Johnny use pain-based questioning to empower Suzie to partner with him? Did he control the meeting by asking questions about what was causing all the pain in Suzie's life? Did he bridge away from a negative statement by Suzie who was ready to end the meeting when she thought Johnny was trying to sell her sales training? Did he not also totally turn the meeting around by stating that now was the exact time that he and Suzie should be discussing sales training? Did he come across as a thought leader who has all of the key industry statistics available at his fingertips? Did he even come prepared with an article that he himself had written? Our boy has set the stage. He has empowered Suzie to move forward and partner with him. But will Suzie ask Johnny how he can help? Or will her sinus headache come roaring back and ruin everything? Damn, waiting is painful. In fact, let's close Act Three with Tom Petty's "The Waiting Is the Hardest Part" blaring out of Suzie's boombox.

CHAPTER SUMMARY

I. After you uncover the pain and enhance it, the next step is to sell against the pain (or develop a tailored solution to ease the pain). You can start to sell against the pain with a methodology called pain-based questioning, or PBQ.

II. PBQ involves asking questions that elicit thoughts, feelings, and actions from the prospect.

   A. The purpose of this questioning is to align your thoughts, feelings, and actions with those of your client.

   B. While uncovering the pain involves asking questions to find out what is keeping a customer or prospect up at night, pain-based questioning takes questioning to the next level. The questions are meant to dig deep, to open a door to a discussion about what else the prospect could be doing or how you might play a role. This line of questioning could potentially lead to multiple solutions that you can provide a prospect via your products or services.

   C. What types of questions qualify as PBQ questions? If a company has been performing very poorly, you may ask:

      1. What are the main factors to your sales decline?

      2. Do you think you need to do a better job of targeting prospects?

      3. How do you target prospects now?

      4. If I could solve one sales or marketing problem that you are facing right now, what would it be?

      5. Pain-based questions are probing in nature and typically start off with, "Is it true that. . .," or "Why haven't you done. . .," or "Did you ever consider. . ." Probing questions elicit much deeper responses.

III. Another characteristic of pain-based questioning is that it empowers the prospect to make a decision. The questions create needs and convince a prospect that she must have what you're offering. Rather than being forced into a decision, a prospect is more likely to accept your solution and feel positive about it if she feels like she's making that decision on her own. You want to ask questions that make it seem logical for the prospect to say "yes." Don't say, "My company has a great solution for you." Rather, ask a question: "If I could show you a way to open doors in companies you haven't been able to pursue before, would that be of interest to you?"

IV. Personalize the questions when possible. Ask your customer how *she* feels about a situation as opposed to how the *company* feels about it. People are more likely to react positively when they feel that they have a personal investment in the situation. For example, instead of asking, "Do you think your company needs to do a better job in targeting prospects?", you should ask, "Do you think you need to do a better job in targeting prospects?"

V. An important public relations technique also used in selling is controlling the interview, which includes bridging back to your key messages. In public relations, we teach senior executives how to control the interview with a reporter. When you go on a sales call, you want to control the meeting and keep it on track to make sure that you're progressing toward your end goal: the sale.

VI. You can also control the interview by becoming a thought leader, being knowledgeable not only about your products and services, but about your client's industry and issues. How can you do this?

    A. Research the company before meeting with the prospect. The company's Web site, as well as a search on articles about the company via the Internet, will provide you with a wealth of information.

    B. Research the industry issues. Again, you can use the Internet to find out more information about the prospect's industry in general, and specific issues that are affecting the industry.

C. Write down a few critical facts and figures about the company and the industry before you meet with the prospect. Mention some of these facts and figures during the meeting.

D. Write an article about an industry issue that is bylined by you and published in a trade publication or local business publication. Showing the article to the prospect will immediately create a new level of credibility for you and differentiate you from other salespeople.

VII. Listening skills are as important as knowing what types of questions to ask. As a matter of fact, you need to listen to the prospect in order to ask the right questions. How do you listen well?

A. Let the prospect talk; keep quiet!

B. Never interrupt.

C. As you listen, think how you can address or solve the issues that the prospect is talking about.

D. Allow the prospect to explain how your company's products or services can solve a problem.

E. Repeat what's been said to you to show the prospect that you understand what was communicated.

CHAPTER 4

Getting the Commitment
(Healing the Wound)

So we've come to a very interesting crossroads: the legendary moment of truth for all salespeople. Questions are racing through our minds:

- Will she or won't she? We sure hope so.

- Have we demonstrated our knowledge and relevant experience? Yup.

- Have we uncovered and validated the pain? Unquestionably.

- Have we made it worse? Amen, brother.

- Have we taken the prospect completely out of her comfort zone? Absolutely.

- Have we read her silent signals and reacted accordingly? Seemingly so.

OK, how do we now empower the prospect to move forward with us?

We do it with one very simple, but profound, question. "If I can provide you with a solution to your problem, would you be willing to move forward with me?" Wait for an answer. If the prospect responds positively and feels the vibes are good enough, go ahead and try to close the deal. Alternatively, if there are still facts and figures you need to move to the close effectively, ask for the pertinent details, and then set a date and time to come back for a final meeting. If she doesn't respond positively, well, there's always that next prospect.

Actually, you need to use your sixth sense at this stage if you're receiving mixed signals from the prospect. On the one hand, it is possible that no matter what you do, there's no hope. When should you say when? We address this in the next couple of pages.

It *is* sometimes possible to obtain a commitment at the end of a single sales call. In fact, because of budget constraints and rising sales costs, many more senior sales managers are exploring methods to close on a first call. Some include:

1. Look at the cost-benefit ratio of a sale. (The dollar amount of the sale will determine the number of sales calls. The bigger the upside, the more of an investment a senior sales manager will be willing to make.)

2. The traveling time involved. (Is the sales call down the street, or does it require two connecting flights, a rental car, and an overnight Motel 6 room?)

3. Behavioral clues by the prospect. (Consider both verbal and silent signals. Is a prospect indicating that the next meeting will be worth your while? Is she sending some positive signals that a little more time and effort will be rewarded? Sales managers debrief their salespeople to uncover these critical clues.)

4. Is a proposal needed? (How much time and effort needs to go into the proposal writing? Can it be a cut-and-paste, off-the-shelf proposal, or is the prospect expecting *War and Peace*?)

5. Was an emotional connection made? (Again, this is where the sales manager's sixth sense will come into play and determine whether he thinks that additional time and effort to close the sale is warranted.)

One large manufacturing company we know discovered that its salespeople had an hour or more of downtime between calls. When they took that hour, multiplied it by the number of salespeople in the field and the number of meetings it took on average to close, they were staring at tons of lost time and out-of-pocket expenses. Once they'd implemented our 20-minute, pain-based questioning approach, the company's sales force was able to cut their unproductive meetings and schedule an average of two or more appointments per day.

Despite the best intentions of sales managements everywhere, the single sales close is still an anomaly, especially nowadays when the sales cycle seems to be getting longer than rush-hour traffic outside the Lincoln Tunnel in New York City. Bottom line: If a close isn't imminent, and you're not getting positive feedback from the questions we suggested above, pack up your tent and move on. That being said, you do have a couple of options:

- If it's a really good prospect working at a great company, ask if you can stay in touch and periodically check in. Also, begin assembling a database to which you can add her name. We maintain a database of names and addresses that numbers more than 1000. It includes current and former clients, current and former prospects, as well as individuals who might be in a position to recommend our services. Each month we mail them some sort of news item to keep ourselves front of mind. You can, and should, create your own monthly mailing campaign. (We explain how to do this in the final chapter.)

- Hold a post mortem on the meeting (if the prospect is willing). Determine whether her "no go" decision was based on objective or subjective reasons (i.e., no budget money versus a total lack of chemistry, or your credentials didn't impress her, etc.). If the disconnection was subjective in nature, learn from your mistakes and come better prepared next time.

For example, we once had a new business meeting with a technology firm that we thought had gone exceedingly well. The prospect's management team seemed highly engaged and extremely impressed with our relevant experience. Naturally, we were shocked to receive a call notifying us that we'd lost.

We asked the prospect if they'd hold a brief post mortem call with our pitch team. They agreed. During the conversation, we found out that our enthusiasm had actually worked against us. The prospect disliked the fact the we had been interrupting each other to share war stories and ideas. What we thought was passion was perceived instead as disorganization. The team learned a painful lesson, and we as a firm now consciously allow one another to complete a sentence or thought before interrupting.

Getting back to our ongoing story, the CEO not only indicated that she *would* be willing to move forward to a next step, she also told us *exactly* what we needed to put in a final proposal. She wanted our four-step consultative selling program to be factored in, as well as a mentoring and coaching component, and a "train-the-trainer" pain doctor module. While she warned us that there were still two other firms in consideration, we knew we had made an emotional connection because of her verbal and silent signal feedback. We knew we had sold against her pain. And guess what? The pain doctors won the business.

Isn't it interesting that the CEO didn't let on that she had been thinking about retaining a firm to help implement a sales training program all along? It's very possible that we weren't even in the running for the business at the early stages of the 20-minute conversation. We won because we quickly differentiated ourselves from our competition. We not only asked about the CEO's pain, we magnified it. We demonstrated thought leadership by citing chapter and verse about executives who'd failed in similar situations and others who'd succeeded. (Naturally, the latter bunch had had the smarts to retain the pain doctors.) The point is, we accomplished *everything* we needed to in a 20-minute meeting.

THE 20-MINUTE MEETING

The four-step selling process outlined in this book enables you to uncover whether or not you can get a commitment to move forward in 20 minutes.

Over the years, we've worked with many large, medium, and smaller-sized sales forces. On average, we've seen that the typical salesperson makes two face-to-face sales calls per day. That being said, our objective in more recent times has been to make clients' sales presentations shorter and more to the point so salespeople can fit more meetings into their daily schedules. The more face time a salesman gets, the more money in his pocket and the more revenue in the corporate coffers.

I. So how should a 20-minute meeting go? Here's our agenda:

A. **Iron-clad preparation**: You know everything about the prospect's industry, her company, and her role and responsibilities within the company. You make sure that she has the authority to sign off on your contract. If she doesn't have the authority, then who does? Make sure you get to the decision maker, or champion. We explain how to do this later in the chapter. You also make sure you dress appropriately (i.e., casual for a call on a technology firm, and buttoned-up business attire for a financial services firm). When in doubt, call ahead and ask about the dress code. Also, determine the physical layout of the room or office and arrange for any A/V support you'll need in advance.

II. Once the meeting has begun, use the following criteria to stay on track (and on time):

A. **The first five minutes**: Quickly establish rapport and uncover the prospect's pain.

1. Uncovering the pain means finding out what exactly is keeping your customer or prospect awake at night. How do you find out what your customer's pain is? Ask questions:

a) What business problems are keeping you up at night?

b) How are your company's sales? Down? Flat? Up?

c) Why do you think sales are down? Flat? Up?

d) How do you feel about your sales being down? Flat? Up?

e) Do customers understand your company's unique selling proposition?

B. **The next five minutes**: Analyze and validate the prospect's pain. If appropriate, exacerbate the pain.

1. Exacerbating the pain involves risk and is not for every situation. Exacerbating the pain can lead to closing the sale, but it can also lead to losing the sale. Deciding whether or not to take the risk depends upon the following:

   a) The prospect's verbal and silent signals. Read your prospect so you understand how she is feeling.

   b) Your level of rapport with the prospect. If you have a strong rapport with the prospect, you may want to go directly to the close, or you may feel more comfortable in taking risks. Either way, you have to read the meeting.

   c) If you have nothing or very little to lose and a lot to gain, then pour salt on the wound:

2. Once you enhance the pain, use the public relations technique of providing third-party credibility, having others do the "talking about you" for you. You can accomplish this by doing the following:

   a) Showing the prospect published articles or case studies that demonstrate what you or your company has done for other clients.

   b) Showing the prospect a bylined article you have written that was published in a trade magazine.

   c) Verbally explain the case studies if you don't have a printed copy.

C. **The five minutes after that**: Provide a solution to ease the pain.

1. How do you get the prospect to move forward with you? How do you get that commitment? Ask! But don't just say, "Can we move forward?" A suggested way of asking is, "If I can provide you with a solution to the issues we discussed, would you be willing to move forward with me?" If the prospect responds positively, then try to close the deal. If the prospect is hesitant, find out what other information the prospect wants and set a date and time for another meeting.

D. **The final five minutes:** Gain a commitment to move forward.

Is it possible to get a commitment in 20 minutes? Yes! But first you need to be fully prepared. You need to know as much as possible about the company, the industry, the prospect's role, and whether or not she has the authority to make a deal. Make sure you dress appropriately and have any audio/visual equipment you may need.

To illustrate further how effective our four-step, 20-minute meeting process is, we've asked three recently trained "pain doctors" to share their views:

- Jim is a 10-year sales veteran who says that he uses our pain-based questioning process to make emotional connections. Selling services in the construction industry, Jim asks such specific, probing questions as, "Are you looking to grow your business?" He also validates pain and takes it to the next level by saying, "You've mentioned that new companies in the scaffolding business are really hurting you. What happens if that continues?" When the prospect replies, "We'll go out of business," Jim responds with one of our patented "easing the pain" questions, "If I could supply you with a list of buyers who would be interested in your services, would that be of use?" In one recent instance, the prospect responded positively. The meeting took less than 20 minutes, and Jim closed a $6000 deal.

- Helen has been selling insurance for two years. She's closed four sales totaling $19,000 in three weeks using our system. She says there's "... no question buyers are more open to making a commitment" when she applies pain-based questioning techniques. "It quickly uncovers who the decision maker is, and whether he or she is serious," Helen added.

- Ronnie is green as grass. In his first month with a telecommunications company, he had attended a traditional sales training program. "They told me to keep making calls to the same prospect before even attempting to close. I was wasting enormous time," he noted. Then Ronnie participated in one of our pain doctor workshops. "I'm now able to gain a quick commitment (or end an unproductive meeting), and on many calls, I'm moving forward to cement a deal in under 20 minutes," he stated. The key, says Ronnie, is adapting *our* process to *your* own selling style and to practice it again and again. Oh, and by the way, Ronnie was just voted "Rookie of the Year" and won his company's platinum award for best sales record.

HOW TO READ THE MEETING

Just because you come in under 20 minutes, it doesn't automatically guarantee success. To become successful, you have to be brief, know how to implement our four-step process, and, drum roll please, know how to read a meeting. By that, we mean you need to know when a sales meeting is going well and when it isn't. Sometimes, the clues are obvious. (When a prospect falls asleep, odds are you won't get the sale.

Conversely, when a prospect says she's been waiting for your product or service, go directly to the close. Do not pass "Go." Do not collect $200.)

Here are lists of some of the characteristics of a good and bad meeting. See how many you've experienced.

Characteristics of a good sales meeting

- *It's short and to the point.* (When the prospect keeps peeking a look at her wristwatch, cut to the chase.)

- *Rapport is established right out of the chute.* ("You know Eugene Karczewski? I used to work with Eugene. What a coincidence!")

- *You establish credibility.* ("So as you can see, Ms. Hussey, we've been published in numerous trade magazines addressing some of the very same pain points you've raised today.")

- *You uncover and validate pain.* ("So no matter what you do, your sales numbers keep dropping, and the number of incoming calls has dwindled to a precious few. Is that correct?")

- *You present solutions.* ("These case study articles illustrate how we've solved similar problems as yours. Once I learn a few more details, we will come back with a detailed recommendation for your widget issue.")

- *You ask questions.* ("Is the widget issue the only thing keeping you awake at night, or is there something else?")

- *You build value.* ("Our customers look to us as much more than just order-takers. I'm here to be an ongoing consultant to you. It's part of our solutions offering.")

- *You differentiate yourself.* ("So as I've mentioned, we're uniquely positioned in not just helping companies sell more widgets, but crucially, counseling those companies who, like yours, are trying to move up-market and be seen as more of a widget-solutions provider.")

- *You empower the prospect.* ("If I could provide the names of companies and people within those companies who might be interested in buying your widget consulting services, would that be of interest?")

- *You answer the prospect's concerns.* ("Not only can we install a widget output thingumajig, we actually hold a patent on the software.")

- *You request action.* ("So assuming that I can provide a tailored solution to the pain points we've discussed in the past 20 minutes, would you be willing to move forward with me to the next step?")

Characteristics of a bad sales meeting

- *No emotional connection is made.* ("So why are we having this meeting again?")

- *An indifferent or distracted prospect.* ("Damn, the stock market's down again. My portfolio is shot to hell.")

- *No chemistry.* (Verbal clue: "Well, you've told me everything about who you are and what you'd do, but you didn't ask me a single question!" Silent signal clues: person folds arm, frowns, and turns away from you. See the section on silent signals in Chapter 1.)

- *Confrontational mood.* ("I was downsized by your consulting firm when I worked at XYZ Corporation. Can't tell you how that ruined my life.")

- *No demonstrated expertise.* ("Look, Mr. Hershberg, you're a nice guy and I admire your company, but I need someone who understands financial markets. All you've talked about is managing large data. I could care less about large data.")

- *No decision makers in the meeting.* ("Well, this is fascinating stuff Ms. Whitman. I'll be sure to pass it along to my counter- parts in marketing. They're the ones who do the vendor hiring, not me.") You need either a decision maker or a champion in every meeting. We show you how to create a champion at your customer's or prospect's organization later in this chapter.

- *No real need for the meeting in the first place.* ("So maybe we'll solve our sales problem by hiring more internal talent, or maybe we'll go outside to someone like you. Who knows?)

- *You empathize with a prospect instead of exacerbating the pain.* ("Geez, that's terrible, Lee. I sure hope things start getting better. Everywhere I go, I hear similar stories.")

DETECTING THE SERIAL PROSPECT

Remember the infamous Ted Bundy? How about Jeffrey Dahmer? Jack the Ripper? All three were notorious serial killers. Although not nearly as lethal, there are such predators in the world of sales. We call them "serial prospects." And they're out to do one of two things: Pick your brain, or use up your time. Either way, they win and you lose.

It seems like serial prospects have come out of the woodwork since the April 2000 market correction. Speaking from experience, we've heard from, and met with, hundreds of these pests. They'll either call you or take a call from you. They'll express interest in your services. They'll spend an hour or more with your top people on an initial sales call. They'll agree to a meeting, or two, or three. They'll always ask for a proposal, or two, or three. They'll always say they have a budget. And then they'll do one of several things:

1. Drop off the face of the earth and never return your subsequent phone calls.

2. Tell you that things have changed within the corporation and they no longer have a need for your services.

3. Take your ideas and implement them themselves.

4. Use your ideas to initiate a request for a larger proposal.

One of our all-time favorite serial prospect stories occurred last year. It began when we were contacted by the vice president of marketing for a company that produced computer peripherals and accessories. He seemed like a very nice guy. He said that his company had been working with a large agency for seven years and had grown disenchanted. He confirmed that they were only considering a small number of firms, possessed a considerable budget, and wanted to make a quick decision. It sounded too good to be true, and sadly, that's how it turned out.

Jumping to the bait, one of our senior people took the prospect out for dinner to get better acquainted. He provided lots of insight into what was needed. Next, he suggested he come over to our offices for a working lunch to give us a more thorough briefing. Naturally, we paid for both dinner and lunch.

Next, we were asked to pull together a detailed proposal. We were told that we and the other finalists would be presenting to this VP and the company president on a Monday. A decision would be made by the end of the week.

We spent hours and hours brainstorming ideas and pulling them together into a comprehensive presentation. We rehearsed and rehearsed.

When we entered the conference room, we saw the competing agency materials scattered across the table. (That's always a bad sign and indicative of the fact that the prospect has no respect or regard for the confidentiality of the search.) During the meeting, we found out that the prospect company president and the head of the incumbent agency were very close and actually vacationed together. (Not a good sign either.) Anyway, we had what we thought was an excellent meeting. We left with smiles and high fives all around. The VP of marketing told us we had done very well with his president.

Then we waited. There was no word back from the VP of marketing at the end of the week. There was no word from him the following week, either. We tried calling, but got no response. About three weeks later, one of us happened to pick up the latest issue of our industry trade magazine and read, "Company XYZ Initiates RFP Process." We were livid. The bastards had picked the brains of three or four agencies, pulled together the outline of what they felt they needed in the way of public relations ideas, and then opened the search up to the entire industry. Long story made short, the serial prospect ended up staying with the incumbent agency. (Those personal ties between the two presidents must have been something very special.)

Serial prospects can kill your morale, sap your time, and steal your creative ideas. There are, however, some simple steps to avoid them:

1. Ask for a definitive decision timetable. (If none exists, that's your first warning sign.)

2. Find out how many other firms are competing for the business. (We seldom compete if there are more than three or four other firms.)

3. Determine who is making the final decision. (This is a biggie. Don't waste your time with someone who has no power unless he or she can be your champion.)

4. Determine whether the prospect has the budget to move forward with you. (Ask if they've allocated a fee for your services. If the prospect is too vague, this might be another red flag.)

5. Don't accept countless meetings. If you can't close after a second or third meeting, it's probably a good indication that you're dealing with a serial prospect. (With one prospect, there always seemed to be just one more meeting. Finally, we said enough was enough and refused to attend the eleventh session.)

6. Ask for mutual respect when it comes to your time. (By that we mean, if a prospect asks for a proposal overnight, ask

them to make a decision in the same time frame. Better yet, buy yourself more time to submit something. We're still waiting for an answer to a major proposal we submitted to a large consumer products company five months ago!)

7. Be selfish with your out-of-pocket expenses. Serial prospects love to be wined and dined. Make sure your antenna is properly adjusted before taking just anyone out for lunch or dinner.

8. If you are submitting a proposal, protect your ideas with a service mark that reads, "All ideas contained in this proposal are the property of (your company)." While it's a long shot, our lawyers tell us this wording will protect us if we should see a serial prospect walk off and use our ideas.

9. Last, but not least, know when to say when. The more times you run into serial prospects, the better you are at sniffing them out. If you're not progressing fast enough, cut your losses, and move on.

CHAMPIONS CAN SOLVE THE SERIAL PROSPECT DILEMMA

A champion can help you sell your product or services to a prospect. But, finding and nurturing a champion is an art form in itself. In fact, it's not too dissimilar from the way in which a reporter uncovers and nurtures a source for an article.

In today's complicated, financially-challenged business landscape, an internal company spokesperson can be a huge asset to you. In addition to finding someone who will speak highly of you, a champion can represent you in final decision meetings where you're not invited to attend (frustrating as hell, but all too common).

We have a real champion within one of our larger clients who absolutely adores us and is constantly mentioning our firm's name when he comes in contact with other marketing types within the organization. We get all sorts of referral business through him. But it didn't happen overnight. We've had to demonstrate our abilities. But once we did, we made a point of wining and dining this individual to make sure that he knows all about us and would feel comfortable recommending us when we weren't present.

Dick Harte's got a great champion story that dates back to the late 1980s and involves one of America's largest insurance companies. I'll let him tell it. . . .

> *A top insurance industry executive attended one of my smoke cessation programs that involved using visual imagery and relaxation to get people to quit. He came away thinking his sales agents could benefit from the same kind of techniques.*
>
> *At a follow-up meeting, this guy put me in touch with the head of his agency, who, in turn, introduced me to his VP of sales. This is the person who would become my champion. After our meeting, he suggested that the best way to get the parent company's business might be to do a test model with his group of agents.*
>
> *The results were little short of awesome. The training group outperformed the other one by orders written, percentage of quota filled, and earnings. The trained sales agents increased earnings by 103 percent, while the control group had an increase of only 43 percent. The trained sales agents also increased the number of insurance policies sold by 21 percent. The control group actually had a decrease of 25 percent.*
>
> *The VP took the results back to senior management and sold in my entire program. The rest is history. I went on to train sales agents in California, New York, New Jersey and Pennsylvania and earned over $300,000 in the process. It never would have happened without my champion.*

So how can *you* get a champion on your team?

1. Find someone who you can make look good to the decision maker at the prospect company (as you'll see Johnny do with Suzie in "*The Pain Doctor*") or someone who can make *you* look good to the decision maker (as in the champion we described above). Here's how: determine who controls the budget in the prospect's company. A good place to start is either with the human resources department or the CEO's administrative assistant. *(Authors' note: The latter almost always knows the inner workings of the company and sometimes can play the role of champion as well.)*

2. Find someone who has the collective ear of decision makers at the prospect company. (Be nice to everyone. You never know who's connected to whom. But don't waste time with anyone who isn't a decision maker, unless he or she can be your champion.) Identify the person who has a vested interest in your services (i.e., a corporate communications manager for PR, a VP of sales for sales training, an HR manager for stress management programs, and a product manager for widgets).

3. Find someone with whom you make an immediate emotional connection. (You and the champion should have an easy-going relationship. You should like each other and want to make each other succeed.) Take this person out to lunch and pick his or her brain. Case in point—at a recent first meeting with a prospect company, Dick listened as the various sales managers debated the gaps that existed between headquarters and the field. Having done his homework, Dick knew that two of the managers had once worked in the field. He set up a cocktail rendezvous, picked their brains, and presented course material that resonated with everyone.

4. Arm the would-be champion with examples of your work so that he, in turn, can pass it up the food chain.

5. Find a proper way to thank and nurture the champion throughout your relationship.

Got it? Good. Now go forth and sell.

One word of advice: try our approach for the next 30 days. (See the final chapter for your personal 30-day blueprint.) Evaluate the process after that time frame. See if you haven't made more contacts. See if you haven't increased the number of prospect commitments to move forward. See if you haven't gotten a whole new perspective on selling. See if we don't charge twice the list price for our next book.

THE PAIN DOCTOR—

Act Four

Setting: The main reception area of Big & Large, Inc. Sunlight is streaming in through huge plate glass windows. Suzie and Johnny have been chatting away since leaving Suzie's cubicle a few minutes earlier. The curtain rises, lights dim. Enter Suzie and Johnny from stage left. Boy, do we love this playwriting stuff.

SUZIE: So yeah, I usually pop between three and four Tylenol Sinus capsules a day. I find that they help me sleep after my ice hockey games. Usually, I won't get home until 1:00 or 2:00 in the morning, so those babies really help me get my three or four hours of sleep each night.

JOHNNY: Three or four hours? That's all?

SUZIE: Oh yes. It's fine. That's all I need.

JOHNNY: Did you ever think the lack of sleep might cause the sinus headaches?

SUZIE: Nope. That's not the reason. Not at all. But it's fine. I'm fine. Listen, I have to go now. Let's get back in touch real soon, OK? *(Suzie pushes her pen toward Johnny.)*

JOHNNY: Look, Suzie. You've got some serious pain that has to be addressed right now; personal and professional pain. Now, I can't help with the headaches and the insomnia, but I can help with the poor sales. Can I ask you one simple question?

SUZIE: Fire away.

JOHNNY: If I could show you a way to solve the poor sales numbers, would you consider moving forward with me and considering me as your partner?

SUZIE: I guess. But I'm not ready to commit.

JOHNNY: I'm not asking you to. I'm asking you to give me a little more information today so that I can come back in a week or so and show you *exactly* how you and I can work together to connect with your customers in different ways. Ways that will enable them to break through. Ways that will impact your sales numbers. Ways that will make you look good to your management.

SUZIE: Fine. But I need the sales force to understand how to sell to a higher-level decision maker.

JOHNNY: Understood.

SUZIE: And if we're going to do this, and it's still a BIG "if," Johnny, I will also need a train-the-trainer program for a group that's trained in the new selling methods to pass the techniques along to my sales force across the Americas.

JOHNNY: Got it.

SUZIE: And I need some sort of mentoring and coaching to be put in place. Smudnoff and the rest are pretty beaten down from a morale standpoint, so we need to instill some positive energy and make sure positive behavior is reinforced, best practices are shared. You know what I mean.

JOHNNY: I know exactly what you mean. Can we keep talking?

SUZIE: Let me check my Palm. Damn. Where's my Palm? I know I packed it this morning. Ummmm. All right. Let's do a real, and I mean real, quick lunch in the cafeteria.

(Lights fade. Curtain comes down. Note how Johnny empowered Suzie to move forward. Note also how Johnny got Suzie to agree to partner with him if he could deliver a specific, tailored solution. Note how Suzie warmed to the task and provided Johnny with the information he needed to come back and close. Did you also note Suzie's evasiveness when Johnny suggested a possible connection between her nightly insomnia and the chronic headache attacks?)

Our boy has accomplished everything he had set out to do. In a 20-minute session with Suzie he followed our four-step process to a "T." He opened a gaping wound, poured just the right amount of salt on it to increase the pain, and then, just when it seemed like poor Suzie had reached her breaking point, Johnny eased the pain. If we have anything to say about it, Johnny will be walking away with an order before the book ends.

So as we leave our virtual theatre seats, we can hear the uplifting melody of Johnny Rivers' *"I can see clearly now"* blaring through the speakers.

CHAPTER SUMMARY

I. How do you get the prospect to move forward with you? How do you get that commitment? Ask! But, don't just say, "Can we move forward?" A suggested way of asking is, "If I can provide you with a solution to the issues we discussed, would you be willing to move forward with me?" If the prospect responds positively, then try to close the deal. If the prospect is hesitant, find out what other information the prospect wants, and set a date and time for another meeting.

II. Is it possible to get a commitment in 20 minutes? Yes! But first you need to be fully prepared. You need to know as much as possible about the company, the industry, the prospect's role, and whether or not she has the authority to make a deal. Make sure that you dress appropriately and have any audio/visual equipment you may need. Here's how a 20-minute meeting should work.

A. 0–5: Establish rapport and uncover the prospect's pain.

B. 6–10: Analyze and validate the pain. If appropriate, exacerbate the pain.

C. 11–15: Provide a solution to ease the pain.

D. 16–20: Gain a commitment to move forward.

III. Avoid serial prospects! You'll recognize serial prospects when they never return your calls, or they tell you that things have changed and they no longer have a need for your services, they take your ideas and implement them themselves, and/or they use your ideas to initiate a request for a larger proposal.

IV. If you can't meet with the decision maker who can sign off on your proposal or solution, make sure the person you are meeting with can become a "champion." In other words, make sure that that person is willing to take your ideas to the decision maker and speak on your behalf.

CHAPTER 5

Using Persistence and Imagination to Close More Deals

How many times have you heard the following axiom? "Success has to be earned." And have you heard this one? "In order to succeed, you must first learn how to fail." How about this one? "Success is 10 percent inspiration and 90 percent perspiration."

There are probably dozens more. The point is that, for most of us, success doesn't come very easily or very quickly. How many articles have you read about some multimillionaire entrepreneur who failed three or four times before finally getting it right? Bottom line: Without persistence and imagination to drive it, our four-part selling process won't get you out of the starting block. You *must* master both in order to succeed.

The pages of history books are sprinkled with examples of men and women who failed time and time again, before finally succeeding. Look at U.S. Grant. As a young man, he was court-martialed out of the army for drinking. Afterwards, he failed at a variety of businesses before finding himself dependent upon his father-in-law for a menial job at a tannery. Once the Civil War erupted, however, and he was given the opportunity to lead men into battle, Grant proved to be a military genius.

What about Harry Truman? Dead broke and destitute at the age of 40, Truman turned things around, became a U.S. senator, and later, one of the more successful presidents of the twentieth century. FDR and JFK are two other examples. Both overcame huge physical problems to rise to greatness.

The sports pages also provide many examples of individuals who overcame some sort of adversity or physical hardship. Wilma Rudolph suffered from polio as a child but eventually became an Olympic sprint champion. Jim Abbott was born with only one hand, but persevered to become a major league baseball pitcher. Monty Stratton lost a leg in a hunting accident, but returned to pitch in the big leagues.

There are many, many other examples.

What each of these people shared was their persistence. They saw their handicap or situation in life not as an obstacle, but as a challenge. They also, undoubtedly, shared another similar trait: vivid imaginations.

Successful people have an *extraordinary* ability to imagine. They feed themselves encouragement by imagining a desired action before it ever occurs. Consider these examples:

- USSR Olympic weightlifting champion Vasily Alexeyev said he routinely visualized himself lifting 640 pounds of dead weight in his *mind* before the competition began.

- The late baseball great Ted Williams often visualized himself hitting a home run *while he was kneeling* on the on-deck circle (and would tell a teammate that he was going to hit a home run before doing so).

- Golfing legend Jack Nicklaus imagines every shot. He actually sees the flight of the ball and where it lands in his mind's eye.

In fact, when great athletes are performing at their peak levels, they speak about "being in a zone." They literally are imagining a pitch, or a pass, or an opponent's move before it actually happens.

While we may not be able to help you become an Olympic athlete or a finalist at Wimbledon, we can help you use persistence and imagination to become a better, more successful salesperson.

One quick clarification before we get started. Some people confuse persistence with willpower. They are not the same thing. When we speak of persistence, we're not talking here about gritting your teeth and blowing through brick walls with sheer brute strength. What we're talking about is blowing through that wall in your mind, and imagining yourself on the other side of it.

Imagination, in fact, is much more powerful than willpower, according to Dr. Emile Coue, the father of autosuggestion. Dr. Coue said that when imagination and willpower come face to face (which is a bizarre thought), imagination wins all the time.[1] For example, you may say you want to quit smoking, but if you can't imagine yourself saying, "no thanks" when a butt is offered to you, you'll never succeed. Chances are you won't become a successful performer on stage if you can't first imagine yourself up there belting out Frank Sinatra's "Summer Wind."

Successful people, by the way, don't focus exclusively on the final rewards. They devote time to planning and reinforcing all the necessary action steps they need to take along the yellow brick road. They unconsciously give themselves specific action suggestions. These suggestions, in turn, inspire vivid images of the super salespeople performing all the daily and weekly steps that will culminate in the big sale.

Remember this: The ability to create and hold a vivid mental image for as little as 15 to 20 seconds a day is fundamental to being successful at persistence. (We show you how to do it in a section coming up.) For example, whenever our new business team is preparing for a major pitch, we ask them to visualize a headline in our industry trade magazine that reads, "XYZ Corporation Hires Peppercom." We ask them to hold that image in their minds as long as possible and to come back to it during the course of the pitch.

Our concept is deceptively simple. When you understand your specific goals and can visualize them in your mind, you will persist toward achieving that end result. You'll have a much higher success rate than someone who cannot or will not use imagination to persist.

MASTERING PERSISTENCE
AND IMAGINATION

Are you ready to learn? Good. Let's start with our six-step program for learning persistence and imagination.

Step one: check for vague, long-term goals

What happens every New Year's Day? Besides the hangover, we mean. Bingo, everyone is making their New Year's resolutions. Some people say they want to lose weight. Others pledge to stop smoking. The lonely hearts vow that they'll find a way to meet that special someone. Sadly, most never achieve their goals because they never create action plans to get them there. They remain in neutral because they feel helpless. Others fail because, well, they've failed so many times in the past, they believe they'll probably just fail again. In step one, we'll find out exactly what your sales goals are and what (if any) specific daily or weekly actions you are taking to accomplish those goals. Here's how you start:

- Make your goals positive. ("I am a better salesperson.")

- Make your goals simple and brief. ("I close one more prospect this quarter.")

- Make your goals realistic. ("I set one more prospect meeting a week.")

- Make your goals measurable. ("I set a meeting with the senior decision maker at Blooey & Hooey.")

- Put your goals in the present tense. ("I am setting a meeting with Blooey & Hooey today.")

- Make your goals rewarding. ("I feel great when I call on a new prospect.")

Here's a quick exercise for you to do. Choose a personal, sales-specific goal and write a specific action suggestion that meets the six criteria listed previously:

_____

_____

_____

_____

Step two: do an honest assessment

Our world is becoming increasingly cluttered with the superficial and the artificial. Politicians say one thing and do the other. (How about George H. W. Bush saying, "Read my lips. No new taxes." Or, to be bipartisan, how about Bill Clinton exclaiming, "I did not have sex with that woman!") With role models like these, is it any wonder that we say one thing and do another? Lots of us say, "I'm starting a diet tomorrow," or "I hate this job. I'm looking for a new one tomorrow." Then, we do nothing. Tomorrow never comes.

But how often do we examine the actions we're taking (or not taking) to reach our goals? Do we feel happy, sad, frustrated, or angry about the actions, or lack thereof? Step two of our process enables you to drill down and get in touch with your feelings. We'll have you tell us what images come to mind when you think of the actions you've taken (or haven't taken). To move from "make-believe" to "real-world action," you have to get in touch with your feelings about what you're *actually* doing; not what you *say* you're doing.

The next question we ask you to answer is this: What do you really want to get from accomplishing your goal?

If you're a female reader whose goal is to lose weight, you might respond by saying, "I want to be 10 pounds thinner so I can once again fit into that black evening dress I bought last year."

Fine. That's a vivid goal.

By becoming conscious of the thoughts, feelings, and actions associated with vague goals, you can take strides towards becoming much more specific. And that's what this game is all about.

We ask you point-blank if you want to become a better salesperson. We ask you to set specific short-term goals that will improve your performance. In the process, we ask you to identify the specific, day-by-day and week-by-week actions you'll take to achieve the short-term goal. Once you know what you want and what you are willing to do to get it, we can translate your desires into vivid, lifelike images of your achieving the goal and succeeding.

Step three: imagine yourself taking action

Remember those world-class athletes imagining themselves succeeding before they picked up the barbell or smashed a backhand down the line? Well, it's time for you to step up to the plate. Let's suppose your goal is to exercise three times a week. You need to use all of your senses to make it come true. How do you feel as you walk to the gym? Are you sweating? Remember the feelings in your muscles as you pumped that barbell? What about the sounds of the barbells clanging after your third rep? Remember the smells of perspiration mixed with perfume? What about that "pumped up" sensation you had in your biceps? Didn't that Gatorade taste great after a hard workout? How about all those attractive bodies you get to watch in the gym? File those ones away in your memory banks. In short, figure out an image associated with each of the five senses and hold that image for 15 to 20 seconds three times a day.

Let's switch to a sales scenario. Try to recall vividly all the sensations of your last successful sales meeting. Go through a mental checklist. What did the room look like? How did you answer the prospect's questions? How did you provide credible case studies? What methods did you use to uncover pain? If your last sales meeting wasn't successful, imagine what you would do in the ideal sales setting. Picture yourself overcoming objections and building rapport. Imagine the sights, sounds, and smells of the room and the people in it. Repeat the exercise three times a day.

Step four: believe it's worthwhile to persist

Hey, if you don't think this stuff will work, guess what? It won't. Call it the power of positive thinking, or anything you like, but if you don't want it badly enough, you won't succeed. Self-motivation can overcome your reluctance to being measured. Let's face it. This is all about measuring you and your progress against a specific goal. If you can, then your imagination will succeed. If not, well, there's always that tollbooth collector's job on the Garden State Parkway.

Step five: pat yourself on the back

In Chapter one, we gave you some of the self-encouragement phrasing you can use every day to motivate yourself. Plug in your specific goal as well as your specific action plans and rewrite the script so it applies to you and you alone. Encourage yourself. Pat yourself on the back every time you accomplish a goal along the road to success.

Step six: self-talk

"Good, self. Way to go, self. I knew you could do it. You're awesome, self." Hey, if you don't give yourself credit, who will? It's an incredibly important habit to develop because it will impart confidence and energize you for the next big goal.

FIND YOUR QUADRANT

We believe there are four different types of people in this world. We're either gifted or mediocre when it comes to our verbal and written skills. The same holds true for our ability to focus on goals. Some of us can and some of us can't. If you take a look at the following table, you'll see how we've mapped the four quadrants, identified the typical characteristics of each, and identified the end game for each of the four types of people. We've even a listed a few names in each box to give you an idea of where famous people might fit in. (See Table 5.1.)

Agree or disagree with our examples. Think of some of your own. The point is, whether you were blessed with loads of talent or not, you can move into the right-hand columns of our chart, which is where the big bucks are made.

TABLE 5.1

Abilities		Goals	
	Unfocused		*Focused*
Gifted	Underachiever:		Superstar:
	Muddles through.		Uses persistence and imagination.
	Mickey Mantle		Bill Gates, Wayne Gretsky, John Elway
Mediocre	No talent, no desire:		Overachiever:
	"One-way ticket to Palookaville."		Surprises everyone.
	Terry Malloy,* Willy Loman**		Pete Rose, Harry Truman

*Terry Malloy was the character played by Marlon Brando in Elia Kazan's 1954 masterpiece "On the Waterfront." Pressured by the mob to take a dive in a prizefight, the up-and-coming Malloy instead ends up with a one-way ticket to Palookaville.
**Willy Loman is the chronically unsuccessful lead character in Arthur Miller's *Death of a Salesman*.

YES YOU CAN. YES YOU CAN

You can learn persistence. Here's how:

1. You need to learn how to assess your current situation and how to align your thoughts with those of your prospect.

2. You need to set goals that are crystal clear. If you can't explain the goal in simple, easy-to-understand language, you won't be able to visualize it. You need to learn relaxation techniques. Why? Because setting goals will increase your stress level. It will take you out of your comfort zone. It will force you to change and as we noted previously, no one likes to change. It causes stress. And if you can't manage your stress, you'll stop persisting.

STRESS MANAGEMENT TECHNIQUES
FOR SALESPEOPLE ONLY
Proper breathing

The easiest and most effective relaxation technique is based on the simple notion of proper breathing. If your breathing is slow and controlled, you will immediately reduce your stress levels. Here's how to do it:

- Sit down and close your eyes.
- Place your right hand on your stomach and left hand on your chest.
- Imagine a blue balloon in your stomach. (*Authors' note: Blue is a cool, soothing color.*)
- Breathe slowly 10 times using the following techniques:
  - Breathe in through your nostrils and imagine the balloon filling up in your stomach.
  - Exhale and allow all the air to flow out of your body.
  - Repeat to yourself silently, "Relax, relax, relax." (*Authors' note: Repeat the above 10 times counting backwards from 10 to 1.*)
  - The exercise should take three minutes.

Self-relaxation

Try this relaxation technique twice a day for two to three minutes. Do it once in the morning or at noon and once in the early evening.

1. Sit in a comfortable chair with your back supported, or lie down. Focus your attention effortlessly on a spot opposite you, slightly above eye level. Take three slow, deep breaths. As you inhale your third breath, hold it for three full seconds as you count backwards: three. . . two. . . one. Close your eyes and exhale. Repeat to yourself, "RELAX, RELAX, RELAX." Allow yourself to go into a deep, sound, peaceful rest.

2. You will remain relaxed for approximately two to three minutes by counting down slowly from 25 to 1. (*Authors' note: It will help if you allow yourself to visualize or imagine each number being written on a blackboard, or shown on a computer, or any way you can experience the numbers, as you count backwards.*)

3. When you reach the count of one, just count *forward* from one to three and you will awaken refreshed and alert, ready to go about your business in an energetic way.

Your stress reduction action plan

Here are some general steps you can take to add to your life.

Physical changes

- Get enough sleep.
- Exercise regularly.
- Eat a proper diet and avoid caffeine.
- Take a hot bath or shower.
- Find a project around the house that you can do from start to finish.
- Close your eyes for a few minutes a day and conjure up an image of a beautiful, relaxing scene from a previous vacation or outing.
- Don't rely on TV or the Web as a tranquilizer.
- Take time for yourself every day for non-goal-oriented activities.

Attitude changes

- Change your expectations.
- Stop expecting to be perfect both at home and on the job.
- Expand your support system.
- Find a mentor.
- Be objective.
- Have a healthy attitude towards your job.

You can learn imagination as well. Here's how:

1. Sit down in a comfortable chair and close your eyes. (If you like, you can put on some music. We suggest Miles Davis,

Dave Brubeck, or even Sinatra. In fact, Old Blue Eyes is great for conjuring up images.)

2. Imagine a scene that is pleasant for you. (Steve's 17-year-old son, Chris, conjures up a Christmas scene from when he was three years old and surrounded by presents up to his ears.) Anything will do. A beach. The woods. An exciting city.

3. Pretend that your mind is a 35-mm. film projector and you're Steven Spielberg. Zoom in on the pleasant scene. Experience it by feeling, tasting, hearing, seeing, and touching the various people and things in the scene. The more senses you bring into play, the more vivid the scene becomes.

4. Hold that image for 15 to 20 seconds. Allow yourself to be receptive to wherever your imagination goes.

5. After focusing on the scene for 20 seconds, count forward. . . . And a one. And a two. And a three. Open your eyes.

Simple? Sure. Refreshing? You bet. Try it yourself. Were you able to focus for 20 seconds, or did your mind wander? If it wandered, you need to practice again and again until you can get it right.

If you *could* focus on the scene, here's a bunch of different action scenes for you to practice twice a day for the next 30 days. Do these in addition to the sales-specific scenario we want you to work on.

1. Imagine doing something special with someone you like. (Steve likes going out with his wife to a fine restaurant. Dr. Harte enjoys obscure artsy-type movies with his wife.)

2. Imagine participating in your favorite sport. (Steve sees himself wiping out his biggest tennis rival, Greg Drury. Dr. Harte sees himself nailing a hole-in-one on the fifth hole at Elmwood Country Club.)

3. Imagine communicating positively with a good friend. (Steve is reminiscing about his midget football days with "El

Hombre Blondo," one of his best friends. Dr. Harte is remembering his *Animal House* fraternity days with his Las Vegas buddy, Marty.)

4. Imagine making an important sales call. (Steve is in the middle of his meeting with a European multinational, a key Peppercom prospect. Dick is conversing with Dirk from Antwerp. Yes, Dirk from Antwerp.)

CHAPTER SUMMARY

I. Persistence and imagination can help you become a more successful salesperson. Persistence is not willpower. It's not about gritting your teeth and blowing through brick walls with sheer brute strength. Persistence is about blowing through that wall in your mind, and imagining yourself on the other side of it. It's all about self-motivation. Successful people don't focus exclusively on final rewards. They focus on *each* of the steps needed to get there, creating vivid images of each step, or, in other words, using their imagination.

II. You too can master persistence and imagination. There are six key steps that will help you accomplish this. Step one focuses on setting goals that you'll be able to achieve. Here's how.

A. Make your goals positive.

B. Make your goals simple and brief.

C. Make your goals realistic.

D. Make your goals measurable.

E. State your goals in the present tense.

F. Make sure your goals have a reward for you.

III. Step two is to conduct an honest assessment. Get in touch with your honest feelings about the actions you've taken or haven't taken for each step. Are you happy, sad, frustrated, angry?

IV. Step three is imagining yourself taking action. Use your five senses to create a vivid mental picture of a sales scenario. Picture yourself overcoming objections and building rapport with the prospect. You can also imagine any scene to help you practice. Here's how.

    A. Sit down in a comfortable chair and close your eyes.

    B. Imagine a scene that is pleasant for you.

    C. Experience the scene by feeling, tasting, hearing, seeing, and touching various people and things in the scene. The more senses you bring into the scene, the more vivid the scene becomes.

    D. Hold that image for 15–20 seconds.

    E. After focusing on the scene for 20 seconds, count to three and open your eyes.

V. Step four is *believing* that it's worthwhile to persist. You must believe in this and want it badly enough in order to make it succeed.

VI. Step five is encouraging yourself and reinforcing your positive behaviors as often as you can.

VII. Step six is acknowledging your own success. If you don't give yourself credit, who will? This will help boost your confidence and energize yourself for the next achievement.

CHAPTER 6

Becoming the Pain Doctor

Well you've certainly been overwhelmed with a lot of stuff. But, trust us, it's good stuff. Stuff you can use. Stuff that can turn around your personal and professional lives. Stuff that will help you convert those previously impossible sales.

So, here goes. Here's how you can become a pain doctor within the next 30 days *(Authors' caveat: The 30-day time frame does not include weekends, religious, or national holidays).*

We'll start your 30-day plan with a self-assessment quiz because, in order to accurately assess a prospect's pain, you first need to be able to diagnose your own. Answer this one basic question:

Are your sales numbers up or down?

- Up
- Flat
- Down

If you answered *"up,"* congratulations, life must be pretty good. You're happy. We're happy. Everyone's happy. But, now is not the time to sit back and rest on those laurels of yours. Corporate America is littered with the carcasses of companies that have made just such a mistake. Remember Smith Corona? They were a major player in typewriters and word processors. Then, along came the personal computer. Smith Corona decided to stand pat with its existing product line and steer clear of computers. So, guess what? Scrap heap time. So do yourself a favor. Keep pushing. Explore new approaches like the ones suggested here. See if they don't raise your performance to an even higher level. Nothing ventured, nothing gained.

If you answered *"flat"* to the question, wake up. Ask yourself what you're doing differently today from the past. And, don't tell us "it's the economy, stupid." There have to be other things that have changed between the time when you were selling lots of goods and services and today. Regardless of the causes or reasons why your sales figures are flat, the next 30 days are a golden opportunity for you to try something completely different. Our approach.

OK. So you answered *"down."* At least you're honest. But, if you really want to figure out why your sales are down and what you might be doing better, you need to take a very deep dive into your thoughts, feelings, and actions. In fact, you need to be totally honest with yourself about your selection of sales as a career path (we'll assume you'll give it the old college try and stick with sales).

So, whether you're flying with the eagles, stuck in neutral or bringing up the rear, you need to realize the two major reasons why most salespeople aren't successful (or continue to be successful):

1. They refuse to take an objective look at themselves
2. They lack vivid, lifelike goals (remember the Ted Williams, Jack Nicklaus imagination section?)

ARE YOU OBJECTIVE?
TAKE THE "PATH TO OBJECTIVITY"

Mark the response to each of the following six questions you think *best* describes your sales behavior. Be honest with yourself and answer according to how you actually behave, not how you think you should behave.

1. My greatest fear in selling is
   a. hurting others' feelings
   b. change
   c. being rejected
   d. being taken advantage of
2. In sales meetings, I find myself
   a. being a good listener
   b. being a good talker
   c. taking charge
   d. following others' direction

3. I perceive selling as
   a. helping others
   b. an exercise in patience
   c. a competitive exercise
   d. a structured process

4. My greatest fault in selling is
   a. wasting time on a call
   b. using high pressure
   c. hesitating to ask for the order
   d. procrastination in closing

5. The greatest joy I find in selling is
   a. building cooperative relationships
   b. being accepted by others
   c. feeling needed
   d. pleasing the buyer

6. I close sales because of my
   a. thoroughness in preparation
   b. energy level
   c. dedication
   d. popularity

If you circled anything but the first choices in the above situations, you should either do a major attitude adjustment or consider another career path, such as bricklaying, for example. Consultative selling may not be for you.

However, now that you've taken the quiz, we'd like to ask you a question.

If we, as your pain doctors, can provide you with a 30-day plan to make a real impact in your personal and professional life, would you be willing to make a commitment to move forward with us? Excellent. We were hoping you'd say "yes."

So here's what you'll be doing for the next month. Take a look.

Your personal life: Work with us to select one facet of your personal life that you want to improve dramatically in the next 30 days. Choose a topic from our list or select something that we can't even dream of:

- Reduce stress
- Lose weight
- Have better time-management skills
- Join a cult
- Other (fill in)_____

Your professional life: This is where the rubber will really hit the road. Choose one of these suggested areas of improvement, or choose your own:

- Increase the number of sales presentations next month
- Increase the number of sales meetings next month
- Meet with higher-level decision makers
- Increase the percentage of new accounts
- Crack that 800-pound gorilla of an account you've been after for ages
- Build existing customer relationships
- Other _____

ASSESSMENT AND GOAL-SETTING WORKSHEETS

Here's how you get started. These assessment and goal-setting worksheets are intended to help you stay focused on specific deliverables. They lists goals, benefits, obstacles, and the specific action plan you'll need to break through and succeed, as well as your thoughts, feelings and actions. We've filled out a sample version of each and have provided blank worksheets for you to use. (See Figures 6.1–6.4.)

FIGURE 6.1.   SAMPLE
                ASSESSMENT WORKSHEET (MODEL)

1. Situation or Problem to Be Assessed:
Example: New business in my territory is significantly behind last year's and this year's goal.

_____

_____

_____

_____

2. Thoughts (What Is My Current Thinking about This Situation?)
Example: I must be doing something wrong. I'm not selling smart. I'm not planning well, and I need help. No bonus.
Other thoughts: My closing ratio is down.

_____

_____

_____

3. Feelings (How Do I Feel about This Situation?)
Example: I'm frustrated. I'm worried. I'm losing confidence.

_____

_____

_____

_____

4. Actions (What Specific Behaviors, If Any, Am I Taking to Correct This Situation?)
Example: I'm currently working very hard, putting in long hours, with poor results.

_____

_____

_____

FIGURE 6.2.   **SAMPLE
ASSESSMENT WORKSHEET**

1. Situation or Problem to Be Assessed:

_____

_____

_____

_____

_____

_____

2. Thoughts (What Is My Current Thinking about This Situation?)

_____

_____

_____

_____

_____

_____

3. Feelings (How Do I Feel about This Situation?)

_____

_____

_____

_____

_____

_____

**4. Actions (What Specific Behaviors, If Any, Am I Taking to Correct
This Situation?)**

_____

_____

_____

_____

_____

_____

FIGURE 6.3.   **SAMPLE**
GOAL-SETTING WORKSHEET (MODEL)

1. Goals (What Do I or My Company Want to Achieve? By When?):
  Example: I want to reach or exceed my goals this year and set the stage for a successful year next year.

_____

_____

_____

2. Benefits (What Benefits Will I or My Company Derive from Achieving My/Our Goals?):
  Example: My earnings will increase. My frustration will turn to excitement. My confidence will return, and I'll feel a great sense of accomplishment. I'll be in control of the future.

_____

_____

3. Obstacles (What Known Obstacles Are in the Way of Achieving the Above Goals?): Note: Use the formula, "Because of _____, the result will be _____."
  Example: Because I continue doing business the same way, my results are poor. Because I can't think outside the box, my sales remain flat.

_____

_____

4. Action Plan (What Specific Steps Must I Take to Overcome Each Obstacle?) Note: Be specific about time commitments.
  Example:
  - *Become more of a thought leader.*
  - *Improve sales presentations.*
  - *Schedule a minimum of five sales calls each week.*
  - *Generate two referrals each week from my customer base.*
  - *Increase my telephone prospecting.*

FIGURE 6.4.   **SAMPLE**
             GOAL-SETTING WORKSHEET

1. Goals (What Do I or My Company Want to Achieve? By When?):

_____

_____

_____

_____

_____

2. Benefits (What Benefits Will I or My Company Derive from Achieving My/Our Goals?):

_____

_____

_____

_____

_____

3. Obstacles (What Known Obstacles Are in the Way of Achieving the Above Goals?): Note: Use the formula, "Because of _____, the result will be _____."

_____

_____

_____

_____

_____

4. Action Plan (What Specific Steps Must I Take to Overcome Each Obstacle?) Note: Be specific about time commitments.

_____

_____

_____

_____

_____

YOUR GUIDE TO BECOMING
A THOUGHT LEADER

Part of becoming a pain doctor includes your becoming a thought leader. How? Here are some proven ideas:

1. **Write a Bylined Article:** A bylined article does not promote your company or its products or services. Rather, a bylined article positions you as a thought leader or expert on a specific topic in your industry. Think about your industry or your customer's for a moment. What is one very important issue that you can comment on? What industry trade magazine do you read? What magazines does your prospect read? Think about a bylined article for those magazines.

   For example, one area that Peppercom focuses on is the positioning and repositioning of companies. When Philip Morris talked about changing its corporate name to Altria, Steve wrote a bylined article for *BrandWeek*, discussing the pros and cons of such a decision. The article didn't promote Peppercom's services; rather it positioned Steve as an expert on positioning a corporation. The article will, however, include a brief paragraph about the author and how you can reach him or her, which is potentially an excellent way to secure additional leads.

   Think about an issue or problem that you can comfortably comment on for one of your trade magazines, and write a brief outline. Include a case study as an example, if it makes sense, and if it's possible to do so (in other words, if you have the customer's permission). Call the editor of the magazine and propose your outline. If accepted, make sure you ask for the guidelines: How many words must the article be? When is the deadline? Do you want the article e-mailed or sent on a disk? Do you need a digital photo of me? If so, in what format?

What should the outline you submit look like?

a) Headline—suggested title of the byliner.

b) Problem/Issue—discuss the industry problem in the first paragraph or two.

c) Solution—explain the types of solution(s) that readers should know about. You can mention your company's products and services as long as they illustrate the solution and don't sound like an advertisement.

d) Examples—back up the solution with case studies from your company.

e) Biography—write about your expertise. Why are you qualified to write this piece?

2. **Write a Case Study:** A case study could be included in a bylined article, as mentioned above, or it can be a stand-alone piece in one of your trade publications. Again, think about one of the trade magazines or newsletters that you read (or better yet, your customer's newsletter or magazine). Do you have a solid case study (or customer story) that demonstrates the problem that the customer had and how you and your company solved it? We talked about using case studies when you talk to prospects. Well, you can also get case studies published.

   Contact an editor of one of the trade magazines or newsletters that you read, and tell them you have a case study of XYZ customer that clearly demonstrates a unique problem and how you and your company provided a solution. As a result, company XYZ has now increased productivity, streamlined costs, or whatever the desired result is. Make sure, however, that you have permission from the company before contacting the editor. Again, if the editor is interested, make sure you find out the guidelines as discussed in the previous section about bylined articles.

Local business publications and the local newspapers are other excellent outlets to approach. For example, if the customer in the case study is located in Dallas, Texas, contact the appropriate business reporter at the *Dallas Morning News* and the *Dallas Business Journal*. Since the story is in their own backyard, chances are reporters will be interested if it's a compelling case study demonstrating a strong problem-solution scenario. How do you find the right reporter? One way is by going to their respective Web sites and reviewing similar stories. See who wrote what. Another way is by simply calling the publication, asking for the editorial desk and explaining your story to an editorial assistant. He or she will lead you to the correct reporter.

3. **Order Reprints:** Now that your bylined article or case study has been published, how can you merchandise it with your customers or prospects? Get reprints! Contact the publication and tell the person in the reprints department that you'd like to order reprints of the article. They will quote you prices on glossy color copies for different quantities. Find out exactly how long it will take before you receive the reprints because it could take a few weeks. Show it to the customer or prospect on your next call.

4. **Create a Database:** Do you have a database of prospects whom you wish you could turn into customers? No? Then, let's start. Take all of your prospects and put them into a database. Use Excel or any program you are comfortable with. List the contact information, and include a "comments" or "notes" section. Every time you contact a prospect, make sure to update the "notes" section. In addition to calling the prospects, there's another effective way to keep in touch and potentially turn a prospect into a customer—launch a direct mail campaign!

5. **Direct Mail:** A direct mail campaign can be very easy to do, and very cost-effective. We're not talking about an expensive, four-color production. Instead, here are some ways in which you can create your own direct mail campaign. First, remember that database you created? Those are the people who will be targeted in your direct mail campaign.

   The objective of the direct mail campaign is to keep in front of your prospect. Although the prospect may not be ready to hire you today or tomorrow, he or she may be ready next month. Here are a few ways in which you can launch your own campaign:

   a) Mail the reprints of your published bylined article or case study to the database. You may even want to attach a brief, handwritten note stating, "I thought you might find the attached article of interest."

   b) Mail an attention-grabbing pitch letter to the database. (See #6, following.)

   c) React to an article in one of the trade magazines. (See #7, following.)

   Make sure to "soft sell" your database prospect with the mailer. It should be seen as informational, or "news you can use," and not as a direct solicitation of business.

6. **Write An "Attention-Grabbing" Pitch Letter:** Write a one-page letter to a prospect, stating a problem in his or her industry and the solution that your company provides. Start off the letter with a hard-hitting question such as, "Because of XYZ problem that exists in your industry, are you afraid you may lose your job?" Explain the issue in a little more detail, and then follow it up with the solution that your company provides. Don't include every detail. Give enough to whet the prospect's appetite. Think of it as a trailer in a

movie theater. When you see a great preview, you want to see the movie, right? Get the prospect excited enough or motivated enough to call you or agree to take your call when you follow up in a week or so. You may also want to ask your prospects, "What's keeping you up at night?" The point of the letter is to take them out of their comfort zone so they connect with the letter.

7. **Keep on Top of the Issues in Your Industry:** No matter how busy you are, it's crucial that you read the most important trades (magazines, newsletters, etc.) in your industry. It will make you a smarter salesperson, and you will understand more of the pain that your customers and prospects may be experiencing. How much more intelligent will you sound if you can say to a prospect, "Yes, I understand what you're saying. But you know what's really interesting? According to an article I just read in last week's *XYZ Magazine*, the industry looks like it might do such and such."

   Separately, you can also make a copy of an appropriate article and mail it, as part of your direct mail campaign, to your entire database or selected targets on your database. Include a handwritten or typewritten note explaining why you're sending the article. Does the article reinforce a point you made to a prospect a month earlier? Or does the article underscore a problem that your company is qualified to solve?

8. **Learn As Much As You Can about Your Prospect:** Arm yourself with as much information as possible before you contact a specific prospect. In addition to staying on top of industry issues, make sure you're familiar with the prospect's issues. Did the prospect company just announce massive layoffs? Is the company restructuring? Does the company fear a new competitor on the horizon? How can you find the information you need?

a) Peruse the company's Web site; in particular, go to the "Press Releases" section and read the most recent press releases.

b) Go to a search engine, such as Google, Yahoo!, or Lycos, and type in the company's name. Recent articles and information about the company will surface.

c) If it's a *Fortune* 1000 company, go to *www.fortune.com* and click on the *Fortune* 500. Although it says the *Fortune* 500, it actually lists the *Fortune* 1000. Click on your prospect company to find more information. In addition, while you're at *Fortune*'s site, just type in the company name in the "Search" area, and see if any articles about the company surface.

d) Subscribe to a news retrieval service such as Lexis/Nexis or Dow Jones. Although these services are not cheap, they are excellent in retrieving articles about a particular company.

e) Go the Web site of the top trade publication in the company's industry. Enter the company's name and see if any articles come up.

Use some or all of the public relations and direct marketing ideas just suggested, and you'll be taking a huge step toward differentiating yourself and becoming a real thought leader.

THE KEY TO UNCOVERING YOUR PROSPECT'S PAIN

Pain doctors understand that there are several key ways to uncover customers' pain, including the following:

1. **Learn to ask the tough questions.** There's only one way to uncover and sell against pain. You must ask some hard questions.

BECOMING THE PAIN DOCTOR

- Is business bad?
- If so, why?
- What are you doing about it?
- Have you changed your strategies or approaches?
- If not, why not?
- How does your poor performance make you feel?
- Has any vendor come to you with a solution?
- Do you have a clear goal you can share?

2. **Learn to take risks.** If it's appropriate to the setting, be prepared to take risks by exacerbating the prospect's pain. (We provide all of the ways to do this in Chapter 2.) Based upon the prospect's answers, try to connect your arsenal of relevant case studies to her pain. Leverage those case studies to make the prospect feel that you understand them. Be prepared to ask the prospect if she'd be willing to move forward with you if you could provide a tailored solution to her pain.

3. **Use persistence and imagination to solve a prospect's problem.** Follow the techniques and strategies we've provided in Chapter 5. Let's say a prospect likes what you're saying but objects to the price. You use your imagination by sidestepping the objection and saying, "You've got a problem and need to solve it. Other companies in the same situation spend money to fix the problem so they don't lose market share. If I can show you how moving forward with the tailored solution I've presented will provide all sorts of financial benefits over the next XX months, as well as such intangibles as X, Y, and Z, would you be willing to move forward to the next step with me?"

Here's a one-minute exercise you can take to sharpen your imagination skills:

Process: Choose an Annoying and Stressful Problem

(We'll create one for you so you can practice.) You have a 9:00 a.m. meeting with a new prospect, and you're stuck on a train that isn't moving. It's 8:45 and you're in a cell phone dead zone. There's no way to tell the prospect you'll be late.

Step 1: Create the stressful situation in your mind. (Focus on the scene for 20 seconds.) Close your eyes (right now) and imagine yourself on that train.

Step 2: Relaxation training. (Allow your mind to go to a peaceful, relaxed scene.) Now you're lying on a tropical beach sipping a margarita. Reggae music is playing in the background. A warm, gentle breeze is blowing. Phew, we're starting to lose it. Let's get back to reality.

Step 3: Go back to Step 1, and allow your imagination to find the solution to the problem. (Focus on the solution for 20 seconds.) *(Authors' note: Don't ask us what the solution is. It's your problem.)*

Know When to Close and When to Ask for Another Meeting

When you get a commitment from the prospect to move forward, you need to decide whether you have everything you need to close the sale on the spot and begin easing her pain. Otherwise, ask for additional information, tell her you'll need to pull together a proposal and would like to set a follow-up date immediately. Stay in touch during the interregnum. The last point, by the way, is a big one. We were once brought into a pretty significant new business opportunity with one of the few surviving dotcoms. Five firms were being asked to pitch the business.

We had several advantages:

1. We possessed an unbelievable amount of dotcom experience and could write *two* books on our adventures and misadventures in that never-never land.

2. One of our staff had worked for the prospect at a previous agency and knew the business model extremely well.

We spoke on the phone with the prospect for a good half-hour, explaining our credentials and answering his questions. He seemed impressed and enthusiastic. He told us he'd e-mail the RFP and would need our proposal in a week's time. "No sweat," we thought. The team leaders called together a brainstorm, came up with a bunch of great ideas, and wrote a damn fine proposal. We waited for his response. None came. Finally, we picked up the phone and were told we hadn't made the finals. "Why not?" we inquired. "Didn't you like our proposal?" The prospect said that the proposal was excellent. But the two finalist firms had called him throughout the RFP time period and had shown him a level of enthusiasm that we hadn't. "Sorry," he said. "But if we don't click with one of the finalists, we'll be back in touch." Yeah right. We'd lost the business because we hadn't maintained the momentum following the first call. It was a valuable, if painful, lesson.

One other point on those horrid lines that prospects feed you when you've lost a competitive pitch. Here's the one we hear most often and hate the most: "We really liked your team and your proposal. It was very close, but you finished second. If anything doesn't work out, we'll be back in touch with you." While we never end up hearing from them, these lost prospects *do* end up hearing from us all the time. We place them on our marketing mailing lists and our management makes a point of staying in touch with the juicier ones. You should too. Staying in touch, even after you've lost, can pay off down the road.

PUTTING IT ALL TOGETHER

OK. It's "go" time. Time to put everything you've learned from this book into action. Here's how we suggest you start tomorrow, which, as you know, is the first day of the rest of your life.

The alarm clock rings. It's 6:45 a.m. You glance outside. The sun is just rising. It looks to be the start of another gorgeous day. And it will be just that. You've got some important meetings today. You need to be alert, focused, and on top of your game. You head off for the shower.

Once you step into the shower (Ouch! Geez, moderate the water temperature a little, will you?), you begin your self-encouragement routine:

I feel calm. I feel relaxed. I feel in need of a back scrubber. I feel in control. I am calm. I am relaxed. I am in control. I feel safe. I feel secure. I'm letting go. As I let go, all my muscle groups begin to relax. I feel calm. I feel relaxed. I feel in control.

As my muscle groups relax, all negative thoughts and negative feelings leave my body, leaving me with only positive thoughts and positive feelings.

My mind is now open to receive the helpful and beneficial suggestions I'm about to give myself.

Today is an important day for me. I am totally prepared when I visit with new prospects today. My enthusiasm and energy become infectious. I share my knowledge and creativity with each prospect I visit. I anticipate all possible obstacles. I offer convincing arguments to overcome any objections. I establish rapport with each new person I meet. I concentrate on the four-step selling process, knowing that it enables me to gain a clear commitment to move forward within 20 minutes. If I don't get a commitment to move forward within 20 minutes, I move on and find other prospects.

I feel calm. I feel relaxed. I feel in need of a towel to dry off. I feel in control.

After your shower talk, it's time for breakfast. As you eat, you allow your imagination to wander freely and envision all the possible obstacles you need to prepare for. You also prepare yourself carefully for the opportunity to close the sale if the opportunity should present itself. You take extra time to review once again the four step selling process: Uncovering the prospect's pain, analyzing that pain, enhancing it when appropriate, providing a tailored solution, and gaining a commitment to partner with the prospect towards a sale.

During each of the four steps, you imagine following the assessment rules. You are not afraid to align your thoughts, feelings, and actions with those of the prospect. You make sure that, for example, your thoughts are in total alignment before moving ahead to uncover the prospect's. After each meeting, you force yourself to conduct an after-meeting review audit. It will ask you to assess honestly whether you:

1. Established rapport

2. Uncovered the prospect's pain

3. Aligned your thoughts, feelings, and actions

4. Used questions to empower the prospect to move forward within a 20-minute time frame

5. Recognized an opportunity to close in the first meeting (and capitalized on it)

6. Felt great, indifferent, or had some other range of feelings and emotions after the sales call

At the end of each day, you perform an after-day review (your significant other loves it when you do this). Once again, you use your imagination to review the day's events. You look for missed opportunities. You congratulate yourself on all the positive events of the day. Here again, you prepare a self-encouragement talk praising yourself for structuring your day, being prepared, and having a great selling day.

You set the alarm, turn on Letterman, and lay back on your pillow, secure in the knowledge that tomorrow will be an even better day than today.

THE PAIN DOCTOR—
THE FINAL ACT

Setting: *Suzie's company cafeteria. Suzie and Johnny are standing at the end of a long line that is snaking its way towards the men's and ladies' rooms. Suzie's shoveling another Tylenol Sinus capsule into her mouth and glancing nervously at her watch. Bruce Blimpbinder, her CEO, just strolled by. Johnny noticed he shot Suzie a glance but didn't smile. Tom Petty's "The Waiting Is the Hardest Part" is playing on the Muzak system.*

SUZIE: Oh great. I just know Blimpbinder has heard about Smudnoff's not closing that friggin' account. He's pissed. Yup, he's pissed.

JOHNNY: Chill, Suzie. Go to him with the solution we've been talking about. Tell him you've got a training program that will teach Smudnoff and the others how to sell against a customer's pain. So that the next time Smudnoff runs into a brick wall like he did this morning, he'll have all sorts of new strategies and techniques to call on.

SUZIE: There is no *way* I will go over to him now. He has to cool off first.

JOHNNY: So you let me get you the detailed program in a few days, and you set a meeting to walk him through it. Makes you look like you're out in front of the Smudnoff issue. Just imagine how smart and strategic that will make you look to Blimpbinder.

SUZIE: Nah, he'd never sign off on the kind of budget you're asking for.

JOHNNY: Wait. Don't you have budget approval?

SUZIE: Yes and no. For something this big, Blimpbinder has to be cool with it.

JOHNNY: Is there budget money?

SUZIE: Yes, but. . .

JOHNNY: Suzie, if I could show you how the sales team will earn the cost of my training back in just a few months and how you'll achieve all sorts of added value benefits as well, would that make it easier to set a meeting with Blimpbinder?

SUZIE: Perhaps. But I'd need to see it in a cafeteria-style proposal. You know what I mean. One from column A, one from column B, etc.

JOHNNY: Can do. Hey, we finally got to the front of the line. What do you want? It's on me.

SUZIE: Big spender, eh? Just get me a BLT on rye with mustard.

JOHNNY: (*Gesturing to short-order cook.*) Make it two. You know what, Suzie? I think this is the beginning of a beautiful relationship. We really accomplished a lot. Can I get you the proposal on Tuesday? That way you can look it over, call me with any questions, and still have the rest of the week to see the big cheese and show him your solution to the Smudnoff issue.

SUZIE: Get it to me on Monday, and I'll *think* about setting a meeting with Blimpbinder. And by the way, lose the *Casablanca* dialogue. You're no Humphrey Bogart.

JOHNNY: I'm tempted to say, "Here's looking at you kid," but I won't. Listen, I'll get you the proposal first thing Monday, OK? But I'll expect just as quick a turnaround from you. And expect a bunch of calls from me in the meantime asking you questions as I pull it together.

And so, the curtain closes. Johnny has truly partnered with Suzie in her desperate sales situation. Let's reexamine exactly what he did.

- Johnny used his imagination to get Suzie to use her imagination to see his company as a smart solution to the so-called Smudnoff issue.

- He created a champion in Suzie.
- Suzie will now use Johnny's proposal to go into Blimpbinder and make herself look proactive.
- Suzie's demanded a quick turnaround on a proposal, but Johnny asked for a quick decision in return.
- He's moved a lot closer to a sale.

There have been hurdles along the way, and Old Man Blimpbinder may throw a few more wrenches in the works, but Johnny has really done a great job in finding out what was keeping his prospect awake at night and then selling against the pain. Hey, he even sprung for lunch. What a guy.

We fade out as Suzie and Johnny munch on their BLTs with the Beatles' song *"Two of Us"* playing in the background.

CHAPTER SUMMARY

I. How can you become a pain doctor within 30 days?

    A. Make an objective assessment of yourself.

    B. Choose a facet of your personal life that you want to improve in the next 30 days.

    C. Choose an area of your professional life that you want to improve in the next 30 days.

    D. Fill in the assessment and goal-setting worksheets in the book.

    E. Stick with it!

II. Becoming a thought leader and differentiating yourself from other salespeople will help you become a pain doctor. How do you become a thought leader?

    A. Write a bylined article about an issue or problem in your industry that you feel comfortable to comment on.

    B. Write a case study about a customer's problem and how you and your company solved it.

    C. Order reprints of the articles.

    D. Create a database of prospects whom you wish to turn into customers.

    E. Send the reprints with a handwritten note to the prospects.

    F. Create an "attention-grabbing" pitch letter to send to prospects.

    G. Keep on top of the issues in your industry.

    H. Learn as much as you can about your prospects.

III. Don't forget! The key to uncovering your prospect's pain is in learning how to ask the tough questions.

IV. Learn to take risks. Don't be afraid to exacerbate the prospect's pain.

V. Use persistence and imagination to solve a prospect's pain. And ask the question, "If I can show you how moving forward with the tailored solution I've presented will provide all sorts of financial benefits over the next XX months, as well as such intangibles as X, Y, and Z, would you be willing to move forward to the next step with me?"

VI. Practice imagination skills by choosing a problem and going through the relaxation techniques.

VII. Know when to go for the close or when to ask for another meeting.

VIII. After each meeting, conduct your own audit to determine whether you followed all the steps. Did you:

    A. Establish rapport?

    B. Uncover the prospect's pain?

    C. Align your thoughts, feelings, and actions?

    D. Use questions to empower the prospect to move forward within a 20-minute time frame?

    E. Recognize an opportunity to close in the first meeting?

    F. Feel great, indifferent, or have some other feelings and emotions after the sales call?

IX. If the prospect doesn't move forward with you, still add the prospect to your database and keep in touch. That prospect who turned you down today could still turn into a customer in the future.

Afterword

What's Keeping Your Customers Up at Night? is the culmination of years of experience in the field.

Between Dick and Steve, we have worked with sales forces and sales and marketing executives at small, medium, and large-sized companies everywhere. In writing the book, we've tried to borrow from the best and most relevant examples.

That being said, we may have overlooked the specific pain points facing your customer. Or maybe we haven't addressed the specific pain that's keeping you awake at night. That's why we're establishing the *Pain-Based Selling Network,* or *PBS.* It's the first online destination for sales executives to meet and share information about personal and professional pain. In effect, it's a pain community in which members will share symptoms and antidotes.

We'd like to encourage you to participate.

After reading the book, go to *www.peppercom.com.* Click on the *Pain-Based Selling (PBS) Network* icon. Inside, you'll find a section on pain stories where we'll ask you to post your favorite case study. In another area, you'll find a threaded discussion section. Each month, we post a different subject heading. One month, we ask for war stories that address how you "cracked that big account." Another month, we examine the gaps between what you thought was keeping your customer awake at night, and after using our techniques, what actually was. We'll be posting a monthly threaded discussion topics calendar, so you can log on when a particular subject peaks your curiosity.

Once a quarter, we will host a half-hour online chat with special "sales" gurus. One quarter, we'll have a top academic with us to answer your questions; another quarter will feature a leading sales trade publication editor. We might even bring other published authors to chat with you.

We also intend to survey you and other sales executives coming to the *Pain Network* site so we can keep subjects and discussions fresh and lively. The *Pain Network* will also have links to others sites that we think you'll find relevant to your world. Our goal is to make the *Pain Network* a "go to" destination for sharing news and information with your fellow travelers in life.

So log on and start conversing with one another. As we said in the book, we all need to find partners. In this instance, you'll be partnering with other sales executives to make that big sale and become even more successful.

One final note: You'll also find a wealth of bylined articles and case studies on the Peppercom Web site. These are the types of materials you'll want to create yourself to become a thought leader.

We look forward to hearing from you in the very near future.

Endnotes

CHAPTER 1

1. Kurt Lewin is universally recognized as the founder of modern social psychology. Bluma Zeigarnik received her Ph.D. under Lewin's guidance from the University of Berlin in 1927. She experimented with Lewin's thesis that a system of psychological tension is motivating until the intended task is executed fully. Zeigarnik confirmed that goal-directed activity left unfulfilled keeps the psychological system pent up with undischarged tension.

2. John Hartland, M.D.; *Medical and Dental Hypnosis*. Baillere Tindall. 1971. London. Page 199.

CHAPTER 3

1. According to the Occupational Safety and Health Administration, back pain is a disability that currently costs employers $20 billion in workers' compensation costs annually and $60 billion in indirect costs, including lost productivity. Second only to the common cold as a cause of worker absenteeism according to the Bureau of Labor Statistics, back pain accounts for more than 40% of all occupational injuries in the United States that result in days away from work.

2. "On the contrary" is an example of a transitional phrase that helps a salesperson bridge from irrelevant or negative comments to his or her key messages. Here's a list of other transitional phrases you can use in a meeting:

- That's an interesting question, it reminds me of...
- Before I forget, I want to tell you that...
- Let me put it in perspective...
- What's important to remember, however...
- What I really want to talk to you about is...
- What's most important is...
- And don't forget...
- Before we get off that subject/topic, let me add...
- That's not my area of expertise, but what I can tell you is...
- That's a good point, but I think you would be interested in knowing that...
- Let me just add...
- That reminds me...
- Let me answer you by saying that...
- Let me give you some background information...
- Let's take a closer look at...
- That's an important point because...
- What that means is...
- Another thing to remember is...
- Now that you've covered _____, let's move on to _____...
- You may be asking why _____ is true...
- While _____ is certainly important, don't forget that _____...
- As I said...

CHAPTER 5

1. Dr. Emile Coue, *Self-Mastery through Conscious Autosuggestion*, George Allen & Unwin (publishers) Ltd., 1984. 3d edition.

Index

About the Authors

Steven Cody is the cofounder and managing partner of Peppercom, Inc., a top strategy communications firm with offices in New York, San Francisco, and London.

Richard Harte, Ph.D., is the president of Harte Associates, a sales and organizational consulting firm. He has designed sales and management training programs for top corporations worldwide.